ARE YOU
WRONG
ABOUT GOD?

CARL MAPLES

WESTBOW
PRESS
A DIVISION OF THOMAS NELSON

WestBow Press books may be ordered through booksellers or by contacting:

WestBow Press
A Division of Thomas Nelson
1663 Liberty Drive
Bloomington, IN 47403
www.westbowpress.com
1-(866) 928-1240

Because of the dynamic nature of the Internet, any web addresses or links contained in this book may have changed since publication and may no longer be valid. The views expressed in this work are solely those of the author and do not necessarily reflect the views of the publisher, and the publisher hereby disclaims any responsibility for them.

Any people depicted in stock imagery provided by Thinkstock are models, and such images are being used for illustrative purposes only.
Certain stock imagery © Thinkstock.

All scripture quotations, unless otherwise indicated, are taken from the Holy Bible, New International Version ®. NIV®. Copyright © 1973, 1978, 1984 by International Bible Society. Used by permission of Zondervan. All rights reserved.

ISBN: 978-1-4497-8961-9 (sc)
ISBN: 978-1-4497-8962-6 (hc)
ISBN: 978-1-4497-8960-2 (e)

Library of Congress Control Number: 2013905704

Printed in the United States of America.

WestBow Press rev. date: 10/15/2013

CONTENTS

PREFACE

I have heard it said that most people have a book in them somewhere that needs to be written. I wasn't sure that this applied to me until God got my attention a few years ago. I kept reading and hearing how our society was moving away from God and how people were developing all sorts of new and strange beliefs that were contrary to the Bible. God convinced me that I could no longer sit by and watch these people fool themselves into thinking that they were going to heaven. So, here I am, asking a basic question: "Are You Wrong About God?" It's a pretty important question! Your eternal life depends entirely on your beliefs.

I was born in the first wave of Baby Boomers. I grew up in the 1950s and 1960s, a time of great prosperity and peace. Life seemed like it was simple and good back then. In the early 1960s when John Kennedy was President, our society was often called Camelot - a reference to a perfect, almost unreal society. We lived in a society where the vast majority of people in the United States were Christians who attended church and lived by Christian principles. In looking back, I think that our downward slide started in the late 1960s during the time of the Vietnam War. The result of that unpopular war was the advent of the drug culture in the United States, the hippies, the sexual revolution, protest songs, violent protests, and a huge distrust of the United States government. People, especially those in my generation, began to change. We felt that change was both necessary and good.

My generation was known as a generation that questioned the status quo and made many changes which still influence how we live today. During my lifetime, I noticed these changes but didn't really pay too much attention to them unless they affected me directly. It seems that life is always full of urgencies and we don't often have time (or take time) to reflect on what is going on around us. When we finally step back and analyze what is happening, we see that major changes often occur in small increments, making them much harder to notice.

There is no question that our world has changed significantly in the last fifty years. When I was growing up, people would often leave their houses unlocked. We didn't have access to the technology that exists today or nearly as many toys and other gadgets that today's children possess, but we were never bored (a common complaint of today's children). Like most Americans of that time, I lived in a home where the father worked and the mother stayed at home to raise a family. I grew up in a Christian home like the vast majority of Americans. Our society's morality was based on traditional Judeo-Christian values, and the Ten Commandments were posted in many schools and other government buildings. Guys' pants actually covered up their rear ends. All of these things, and more, have changed during the last fifty years, and our society is showing the effects of these changes.

Today we live in a United States society where the divorce rate is about 50 percent, where we have killed millions of babies because of the "Pro-Choice" movement, where millions of children grow up in single parent homes, where the U.S. government and many municipalities have huge financial problems, where greed has corrupted major corporations and caused major scandals, where moral values continue to decline, and, worst of all, where a vast majority of Americans no longer attend church. Why would God continue to bless a nation like this?

One of the most significant changes in America has been a change in attitudes about religion, which has led to a reduction in the percentage of Americans who call themselves Christians. Among those who still consider themselves to be Christians, there has been a decline in the commitment level and a big change in beliefs. Researcher George Barna recently determined that "Casual Christians" are now the largest faith group in America, accounting for two out of every three adults. [1]

So, what is a Casual Christian? Well, it might be more appropriate to call this group "Comfortable Christians". This is a group of people who have adopted a belief system that fits what they are comfortable with. In other words, they have adopted just enough parts of Christianity to help them feel comfortable with their religion. For the most part, these are good people who have convinced themselves that they are going to heaven when they die. People in this group have adopted a religion that is not demanding on their time, behavior, or priorities – yet it is a religion that makes them better people than they would be otherwise. Barna describes the main objective of this group as being a pleasant and peaceful existence.

The changes in attitudes over the last fifty years have led to a desire by individuals to define their own religion by adopting a set of beliefs that comfortably fits with what they *want* to believe. At the risk of making you uncomfortable, how confident are you that your current beliefs are correct? Are you one hundred percent sure that you are going to heaven when you die? Have you made decisions on what to believe without getting all of the facts? Are you willing to accept the risk of inventing your own religion and then finding out after you die that you were wrong? If you are willing to know the truth about God, then you need to keep reading this book. If you already know the truth, do you know someone else who could benefit from reading this book?

A Hindu friend of mine recently told me that "religion is just a matter of opinion". Do you agree with this statement (like lots of people do)? Is it possible that people can find God by looking somewhere other than the Bible? Does it make sense for people to define their own God? Do all religions lead to the same place? Is it possible that God could provide the spirituality that people are looking for? What is more important – how you feel about yourself or how God feels about you? This book will reveal what God says about these questions.

If you are a committed Christian who is striving to be more like Jesus, have you noticed that people have been moving away from organized religion in large numbers? Have you ever wondered why? It is not because people have a problem with Jesus – it is because they have been turned off by Christians (including clergy members). The majority of these people have positive feelings about God and Jesus but negative feelings about church members. They overwhelmingly feel that churches are full of hypocrites who are not concerned about loving people! They are right! Are you part of the problem or part of the solution?

I am writing this book from a Christian viewpoint that will be beneficial for you whether you are a Christian or not. My goal is to present God's viewpoint rather than my own. I hope you will read this book with an open mind. I would like to hear from you about what you believe. At the end of the book you will find information about ways you can discuss the important facts in this book.

The purpose of this book is very simple – to give you the facts that will enable you to answer the question "Are You Wrong About God?" I hope you will be receptive to the information in this book and honest with yourself when you assess your current beliefs. You are the target in the great spiritual warfare that has been going on for thousands of years, and nothing is more important than for you to have God on your side. It is time for us to take the apostle Paul's advice and "gear up" to withstand these attacks and to help us discern the truth:

> "Put on the full armor of God so that you can take your stand against the devil's schemes. For our struggle is not against flesh and blood, but against the rulers, against the authorities, against the powers of this dark world and against the spiritual forces of evil in the heavenly realms." [2]

INTRODUCTION

In this book, we will be looking at what people believe about God compared to what God says about himself. There has always been a tendency for us to make God into our own image instead of accepting the fact that he made us in his image. As we will see shortly, the gap between who God is and who we think he is seems to have grown in the last twenty years or so. People in the United States are moving away from God and the Christian church at an alarming rate, similar to trends we have seen in some European countries. To understand why and how people's religious beliefs are changing, we need to look at some of the changes in our attitudes and behavior over the last twenty years.

How Have We Changed?

George Barna did an excellent job of predicting some of these changes in his 1990 book *The Frog in the Kettle*. As I was writing this, I can honestly say that my first impression was that we are not that much different than we were in 1990. But after further reflection, I can see that the changes that have taken place since that time have been major and have had a huge effect on religion in America today. Here are some of the major predictions from this book: [1]

- People will become more self-centered, materialistic, and selfish with their time.
- Change will be viewed as good and mostly necessary. Religions with established traditions will be viewed as inflexible and unappealing. Institutional loyalty will decrease.
- Many people will view commitment as being too rigid and in conflict with selfish desires. This will affect established religions and the institution of marriage.

- Time will replace money as the most valuable currency. People will avoid activities that are perceived as time-wasters.
- There will be more reliance on self versus others and a greater emphasis on self-control. This will create a reluctance to allow other people and/or groups to tell us what to believe or how to behave.
- Increased focus on self and satisfying selfish desires will also increase the practice of cafeteria religion. People will think they are improving Christianity by changing it. Even devout Christians may attend more than one church.
- We will continue to see a breakdown in the traditional family structure. This breakdown will have far reaching effects as the next generation grows up.
- Trust will be replaced by skepticism. Groups and individuals will be required to prove their integrity.
- People will focus on getting exactly what they want rather than making sacrifices to accept what is available.
- The concept of a single God that is right for everyone will become increasingly difficult for many people to accept.
- Traditional religious denominations are likely to experience reduced membership.

These things have happened exactly as predicted! To summarize all of these items into a single sentence, I would say that there has been an emphasis on the power of the individual and self-control. Many people have become reluctant to submit to or commit to any outside influence. People are changing their behavior and beliefs to fit their own desires instead of changing their beliefs to fit with God's plan for their lives. Sadly, millions of people have moved away from God to focus on their own selfish desires. Why are these selfish desires becoming important? Because our materialistic society has convinced many people that they will be happy by getting everything they want! In reality, these selfish desires only produce temporary pleasure. In some cases, they might make you feel good about yourself as a person. Ask yourself if you have true joy in your life or just occasional happiness. True joy is provided only by having a meaningful relationship with God.

Recent Barna surveys revealed that 66 percent of American adults can be classified as "Casual Christians" and that 71 percent of people surveyed were more likely to develop religious beliefs on their own rather than adopting what a church teaches.[2] A Casual Christian is one who has just enough religion to feel comfortable but not enough to be really committed to it. I believe that many, perhaps most, Casual Christians are not really Christians at all. There are a number of things that lead people to believe they are Christians when they really aren't. Examples are growing up in a Christian home, being sprinkled as a child, believing in God, attending church, and keeping the Ten Commandments. These things mean that a person knows who Jesus is, but he doesn't really know Jesus personally. Being a Christian requires accepting Jesus as your Savior and having a relationship with him.

We just saw that a majority of Americans have customized their own religious beliefs but still aren't committed to them. Are you one of these people? Have you convinced yourself that your beliefs are correct, or are you willing to take a further look at what God has to say about your beliefs? I hope you will make an honest assessment of yourself as you read through this book.

Incredibly, we will see from a number of surveys referenced later that large percentages of Christians hold views that are directly contrary to the Bible. Does this indicate that these people consider the Bible to be irrelevant or does this indicate a growing amount of biblical ignorance? The Barna Group found in 1990 that 58 percent of people who owned a Bible were unable to say who preached the Sermon on the Mount. [3] (By the way, it was Jesus). Given that this sermon is probably the most famous sermon in the Bible, and that it appears in the very first book of the New Testament, wouldn't this indicate that many people who own a Bible are not really familiar with its content? If there is this much biblical ignorance in our society, where are people getting their information and beliefs about God? What is the source for your own religious beliefs?

There have been other major changes over the last twenty years that affect who we are today, such as the impact of technology, credit cards, globalization, terrorism, and the Internet. We can't ignore these as being major factors in how we live on a daily basis. However, none of these things directly influence our religious beliefs. Instead, the increased focus on ourselves has given Satan many opportunities to tell us what we want to hear and make new approaches to God sound attractive and comfortable.

This book will examine some of the beliefs that are prevalent today and identify individual beliefs and tendencies that are behind the move away from Christianity. We will look at specific examples comparing various religious beliefs to what God says about himself. The objective of this analysis is to help you make an informed decision based on God's Word. If you are a committed Christian, this information will help you minister to others.

The desire to develop a customized religion leads to believing things that we *want* to believe, rather than looking for the truth. There is a huge difference in these two approaches! We should not believe theories about God without testing these theories against the Bible to see if they are consistent and complete.

What is This Book About?

So, what can you expect to see in this book? Simply stated, we will identify the truth about God! The truth can be revealed by studying Jesus, who said "Everyone on the side of truth listens to me." [4] As we identify truth, you will obtain a better understanding of Satan's increased efforts to pull us away from God. Satan is a liar, a deceiver, and a counterfeiter of the one, true God. It is important for everyone to learn how to tell whether a theory about God comes from God himself or from Satan.

Here are just a few of the ideas that are being promoted as truth today:

- God is not a being but rather some sort of energy force that is in everything.
- Jesus is not really the Son of God.
- You can define your own god and there are many ways to that god.
- You can find god by obtaining a higher level of consciousness – i.e. finding the god within you.

- There is no such thing as sin; therefore, we don't really need a god.
- Hell and Satan are not real - they are just symbols of evil.
- All religions really are just different versions of the same truths.
- You can get to heaven by being a good person.

These statements are directly contrary to the Bible. But, it is easy to see how they could appeal to our selfishness. You can sign up for a religion in which God is just whatever you want to believe. Not only that, there is no sin, and you aren't really accountable to anyone except yourself! You can make up your own rules and live however you wish. When you die, there is no penalty because you will always be in compliance with your own rules. In fact, you can become a god yourself. This all sounds appealing, but does that mean it is true? Are you willing to bet your eternal life on any portions of a belief system like this?

Regardless of your current beliefs, this book promises to challenge your thinking.

Here are some of the things we will cover:

- The major religions and how they differ
- Why we aren't as smart as we think we are
- How our attitudes are affecting our beliefs
- What we know and don't know about the spirit world
- What we know about God and how different groups define God
- Evidence that supports the existence of God
- Evidence that supports the deity of Jesus
- The capabilities and behavior of angels
- The capabilities and behavior of Satan, demons, and evil spirits
- Spiritual warfare and how it affects us
- Satan's lies and deceptions and how to recognize them
- The coming end times and how to recognize and survive them
- The removal of Christians from the earth (the rapture)
- The New World Order – blessing or curse?
- Is Jesus the only way to God?

This book will identify some of the misinformation about God, explain where to get the answers we are looking for, help us find those answers, challenge our thinking, show us how to survive the spiritual war that is increasing in intensity, and lead us in discerning between right and wrong. My hope is that this information will encourage you to spend more time learning about God and developing a personal relationship with Jesus Christ.

CHAPTER 1:

What People Believe

Like it or not, the decisions that we make and our behavior are greatly influenced by our society and the people we associate with. Without a proper focus on God's Word, we will have a tendency to conform to the modern world. In this chapter, we will examine the current environment in which we live to see how it has changed and why it has created opportunities for new ideas about God.

There is a lot of interest in spirituality in our modern society. Spirituality and religion are related but not really the same topic. The term *spirituality*, when used in this book, means a focus on internal matters of the mind and spirit. For example, participating in a self-improvement program, practicing meditation, or reading a self-help book can improve your mind and your spirit. Spirituality is a way of understanding ourselves, connecting with who we really are, and trying to improve ourselves without necessarily involving religion. The term *religion* in this book will refer to a belief in things that are outside the mind and spirit but that influence your mind and spirit. Religion focuses on belief in a supernatural, sacred, and divine being (or beings) who is greater than all things and is the source of truth. Historically, many religions have developed around superstitions, cultural practices, myths, and legends without necessarily believing in a god.

A person can be spiritual without being religious, but a person who is religious will automatically be spiritual. In practice today, many people use the term spirituality to mean the process of getting in touch with their version of the truth (which often includes belief in some sort of divinity) using whatever path they consider appropriate. Usually the term religion is used more to refer to traditional belief systems that don't allow people to define their own version of the truth.

Are You Going To Heaven?

Did you know that you are going to live forever? Yes, that is really true. The Bible teaches us that your spirit will live forever after your body dies. Normally, this would be good news, but the Bible also teaches that some of us will be in heaven with God and others will be in hell separated from God for eternity. It is up to you to choose how you want to spend eternity.

The vast majority of Americans believe in heaven, but they express different opinions on how to get there. An ABC News poll in 2005 revealed that 75 percent of Americans believe that they will go to heaven and 60 percent believe that both Christians and non-Christians will be allowed in heaven. [1] What do you believe? Have you convinced yourself that you are going to heaven? Are you sure? Lewis Carroll, author of *Alice's Adventures in Wonderland*, said, "If you don't know where you are going, any road will get you there." Do you agree with the belief that there are many roads to God and any road will get you there? Do you think that just being a good person or doing good works will suffice? Do you believe that God is a God of love and he would never send one of his children to hell? Do you believe that heaven and hell really exist?

Look at it this way: Do you have a retirement plan like a pension, IRA, or 401(k) plan? Many of you will answer yes to this question, and even if you answer no, the U.S. government has set up a Social Security system to help you in your retirement years. (Hopefully we will be able to get back some of the money we have paid into the Social Security system.) If you do have a retirement plan, then why do you? Why don't you just take the position that any road will get you to retirement, and you don't need to worry about it? This is obviously a rhetorical question. You can't think just any road will work. If you ignore retirement planning, then you really have no idea of what to expect after you retire. Sadly, many people in the U.S. have not given enough attention to this area.

Does it make sense to plan for the final few years of your physical life and not plan for the eternal life that your spiritual body will experience? If you believe in heaven, does it make sense to say that any road will get you there? I don't think so! If you leave this to chance or choose the wrong road, then you aren't going to be there. Or as Yogi Berra, the popular baseball player and coach, said, "If you don't know where you are going, you might end up someplace else." Someplace else is not a very good alternative to heaven!

Making sure you go to heaven is the most important thing you can do for yourself in your lifetime. Have you taken the steps necessary to get there? Have you focused more on your retirement plan than your post-retirement plan? Are you focused on the present, maximizing your material possessions and enjoying yourself as much as possible? Jesus asks us in Mark 8:36, "What good is it for a man to gain the whole world, yet forfeit his soul?" If you believe in heaven, don't you think it is important to find the truth about how to get there?

The Bible tells us that you can't get to heaven just by being a good person or by doing good deeds! This is made clear in Ephesians 2:8-9: "For it is by grace you have been saved, through faith—and this not from yourselves, it is the gift of God— not by works, so that no one can boast." You can't get to heaven just because your parents were Christians. You can't get there just because you go to church occasionally. The Bible tells us clearly that you can only get there by accepting Jesus as your Savior and Lord. This requires an action on your part! I realize that this statement is highly offensive to many people, but it comes from God's Word.

Don't you think that if there were some way for us to go to heaven by being good, God would have laid out the criteria and the rules somewhere? Without these rules, we would just be guessing on how much good is good enough. Does it make sense that God would give us multiple ways to get to heaven, such as either following Jesus or just being good? God is incredibly fair and just because his requirements are simple and are the same for everyone. All you need to do is accept Jesus as your Savior. When Jesus was crucified, he told the thief on the cross next to him that the thief would be with him in heaven that day. The thief was saved for one simple reason: he trusted in Jesus.

Worldwide Religious Preferences

It is amazing how many opinions there are about God. It is even more amazing when we consider that God defined himself clearly in the Bible so that we could understand him. Sure, there are things we would like to know that he didn't tell us. But there is enough evidence and written information for us to make an informed decision. In spite of this, there is much confusion in the world today about who God is, even among Christians. Some of this confusion is created by the wide variety of religions and some by modern beliefs spawned by New Age thinking or the doctrine of political correctness. It is hard to avoid some of these influences because they show up in popular books, movies, Internet blogs, and television shows.

The world's religious preferences are summarized in Figure 1. [2]

Figure 1 - Worldwide Religious Preferences (2001)

Common Name of Religion	Members In Billions	Percent of Total
Christianity	2.1	30.6%
Islam	1.5	21.8%
Non-Religious	1.1	16.0%
Hinduism	.9	13.1%
Chinese Traditional	.4	5.8%
Buddhism	.4	5.8%
Tribal Religionists & African Traditional	.4	5.8%
Judaism	< .1	0.2%
All Others	.1	0.9%

There are several interesting observations that we can make by looking at this chart. First of all, Christianity and Islam, which are the two newest religions, are also the largest. Christianity began about two thousand years ago and Islam about six hundred years later. These two religions together with Judaism believe in a single being, an all-powerful God (but with significant differences in what they believe).

Second, the next largest single group is labeled "non-religious." This group primarily consists of people who either have no stated religious preference or just don't have any religious beliefs at all. Surprisingly, about half of the people who fall in this group *do* believe in God or some sort of higher power. [3] However these people are classified as non-religious because religion is not important enough to them to cause them to associate with any of the established religious groups. This group is growing in both size and influence.

Finally, we should note that New Age is not listed as a religious group in spite of the influence of New Age theories on modern thinking. The reason for this is that there is no central organization, nor is there a common belief system among all the groups comprising the New Age movement. In addition, most people who participated in this survey actually listed a traditional religion as their primary religion even though they believe in one or more New Age concepts. The New Age movement seems to be able to cross religious boundaries to attract followers.

If you broke these numbers down further, you would see that each group consists of a number of different factions (or denominations) that don't really agree with each other on a variety of issues. How do you think God feels about all the theories that are trying to explain who he is? God has given us the Bible and his Son Jesus so that we can see *exactly* what God is like. Jesus said "If you really knew me, you would know my Father as well. From now on, you do know him and have seen him." [4] If we really want to understand God, we need to focus on Jesus. The things that denominations disagree on seem to be relatively unimportant when compared to the importance of focusing on Jesus.

American Religious Preferences

There is one inherent problem with survey results. What people say and what they do is often not the same thing. Perhaps you have heard the Ralph Waldo Emerson saying, "What you do speaks so loud I cannot hear what you say."

Unfortunately, it is a well known fact that people participating in surveys don't always tell the truth. For example, if you ask someone how often they go to church, they may answer based on how often they *should* go rather than how often they *actually* go. Therefore, we should view some of the survey results as possibly being overstated.

Based on a variety of surveys, the vast majority of adult Americans consider themselves to be Christians, at least based on survey responses. Figure 2 shows religious preferences as of 2001. [5]

Figure 2 - Religious Preferences in the United States (2001)

Common Name of Religion	*Members In Millions*	*Percent of Total*
Christianity	159.0	76.5
Non-Religious/Secular	27.5	13.2
Judaism	2.8	1.3
Islam	1.1	.5
Buddhism	1.1	.5
Agnostics	.9	.5
Atheists	.9	.4
Hinduism	.8	.4
All Others	13.3	6.7

It is not surprising that over three-fourths of adult Americans consider themselves to be Christians. Documents written by several of our founding fathers reflect the belief that the United States was founded as a Christian nation. When I was in grammar school, it was still acceptable to publicly pray in school. It was permissible for teachers to refer to the Bible as part of the study of creation. Most everyone I knew went to church on a regular basis. Christianity was an important influence in our society, and no one was embarrassed to talk about it.

Today, many people who say they are Christians don't even attend church. In fact, you would think that many Christians are not Christians at all based on their actions and their lifestyles. In my 37 year working career, I met a variety of people from across the United States. These were primarily people in business careers, but I think they were a representative sample of all ages and backgrounds. Based on my observations, I would have thought that less than half of them were Christians. A variety of surveys taken by different organizations reveals that the percentage of Americans who attend church regularly is around 40 percent. Given that people tend to exaggerate when answering survey questions, the actual percentage is probably lower. Some experts have placed this percentage as low as 20 percent. In addition, not all people who attend church are serious about their religion. In other words, they give the appearance of being religious, but they don't really have a personal relationship with Jesus Christ.

So, is America a Christian nation or not? Actually, the nation itself cannot be called Christian because we have a separation of church and state in America. What we can say is that the majority of Americans still consider themselves to be Christians. However, just because Christianity is the largest religion in America does not make America a Christian nation.

A study by Lifeway Research in 2007 found that 61 percent of Americans who are *not* attending church believe that the God of the Bible is no different than the gods or spiritual beings depicted by other world religions such as Islam, Buddhism, and Hinduism. [6] Where does this view come from? God certainly doesn't say this about himself! What do you believe? I believe that it reflects the opinions of those who make decisions without gathering the facts.

If we were to look at the trends behind the religious preference chart, we would find that the non-religious / secular group grew by 110 percent between 1990 and 2000 (more than double!). [7] This translates into around 14 million

Americans that were added to this group in just 10 years. The percentage of Americans who call themselves Christians has declined during this same period. The Pew Forum on Religion & Public Life released an updated survey in 2012 that revealed that now 20 percent of Americans can be classified as non-religious, up from 15 percent in just five years. [8] This means that there are about 46 million non-religious Americans.

Another study by the Pew Forum on Religion & Public Life in 2007 confirmed these trends and revealed how many people are changing their religious preferences. [9] This study revealed some alarming statistics:

- Only about 12 percent of mainline Protestants, 16 percent of Catholics, and 36 percent of evangelical Protestants believe that their religion is the one true faith. In other words, the vast majority of Christians do not agree with Jesus' statement that he is the only way to God.
- More than one-fourth of U.S. adults have left the religion they were raised in for another religion or for no religion at all. This does not include those who changed denominations within the same religion.
- Those who say they are not affiliated with any particular religion totaled 16 percent of the population in 2007 (versus 13.2 percent in 2001). For young Americans between 18 and 29, the total is around 25 percent.
- 71 percent of all people who are not affiliated with a religion are under the age of 50. Since about 60 percent of all Americans are under the age of 50, we can infer that younger Americans are less committed to religion than older Americans.
- Two-thirds of American Buddhists are not Asian, and three-fourths say they were converted to Buddhism.

These are disturbing numbers for Christians. We can tell from these numbers that many of the three-fourths of Americans who claim to be Christians are older Americans. This was confirmed by a 2007 Barna study, which revealed that each younger generation has a smaller percentage of people who claim to be Christians (about 60 percent for the 16-29 age group) [10]. As our older citizens pass away, the percentage of Americans who call themselves Christians will continue to decline if the current trend continues. At the same time that we are seeing people move away from Christianity and traditional churches, interest in spirituality is at an all-time high. Many people are moving away from God but still looking for the things that he can provide! Does this make sense?

How do the statistics in this section apply to you and your family members?

There will be consequences to our country because we are moving away from God! God told this to Solomon in 2 Chronicles 7:14: "...if my people, who are called by my name, will humble themselves and pray and seek my face and turn from their wicked ways, then will I hear from heaven and will forgive their sin and will heal their land." God then goes on to explain that he will bring disaster on Israel if they ignore him and turn to other gods. (This is exactly what happened). God's statement applies to any group of people who claim to be his followers. This should be a wakeup call to all Americans!

If you don't believe that our actions will have consequences, then read Jonathan Cahn's excellent book *The Harbinger: The Ancient Mystery that Holds the Secret of America's Future*. This book focuses on some events that are outlined in Isaiah chapter 9. Israel had turned away from God, and God punished them by allowing a foreign country to invade and destroy some of their buildings. The people did not recognize that this was a warning from God, so they became defiant and boasted that they would rebuild bigger and better than before. In other words, they relied on their own strength rather than God's. Their actions and failure to return to God resulted in the ultimate destruction of Israel. This book reveals a number of exact parallels to the events of 9/11/2001 and following. Political leaders in our country actually quoted from Isaiah 9 while issuing a proclamation of defiance. The recent economic recession and collapse of the real estate and banking industries can be traced directly to actions taken by the Federal Reserve immediately after 9/11. Did God allow a foreign attack on our soil as a warning to us that we need to turn back to him? This book makes a compelling case that he did. And, if he didn't, we can look at God's behavior as documented in the Old Testament to tell that such a warning is coming. My fear is that our nation is so disconnected from God that we would not recognize another warning from God. We certainly did not turn back to him after the 9/11 attacks. The number of non-religious people in the country has continued to increase since that time. If you are disconnected from God right now, he is waiting on you with open arms.

The Decline in Morality

It shouldn't be surprising that the increase in the number of people who no longer seem to rely on God is occurring at the same time as a decline in morality in the U.S. If we don't get our morals from our religious beliefs, then where would we get them? Surely we aren't going to rely on the government to tell us what is moral and what isn't. But that is exactly what is happening. Do you believe that when the government says something is legal, then it must be moral?

In the 1991 book *The Day America Told the Truth*, the authors noted that throughout the U.S. about 90 percent of the population said that they believed in God. However, they discovered that people do not turn to religion to help them make up their mind on moral issues [11]. In other words, people believe in God but don't think that he has any relevance for their day-to-day lives. This opinion is supported by the fact that only a minority of the people who believe in God think religion is important enough to go to church on a regular basis.

A 2010 Gallup poll found that 70 percent of Americans said that religion is losing its influence on American life, which is up substantially from just ten years earlier. [12] What has happened in the last ten years? I read a blog recently where an anonymous poster said "Morals are governed by human society, not an imaginary deity." What does this mean? It means that this poster thinks that morals are whatever we want them to be and are totally independent from how God wants us to act.

Do you think it is acceptable to cheat? After all, the Bible does not say "Thou shalt not cheat." The United States government says we can't cheat on our tax returns, but they haven't outlawed all types of cheating yet. Would this mean it is alright in certain cases? One of the benefits of relying on God for daily decisions is that God will give us a conscience that we can't ignore. Certain things will bother us, which will influence us to not do them. However, our society seems to be more concerned with individual rights and tolerance than morality. If enough people complain about something, it will often become legal.

By early 2012, eight states had legalized same sex marriage despite a number of surveys that show the majority of the population is not in agreement with this type of union. Several other states are working on legislation in this area. However, these surveys also revealed that acceptance of same sex marriage is growing, particularly with the young age groups. Where will we draw the line on political correctness and tolerance? Will incestuous marriage be the next thing that we will legalize so that we won't offend anyone? We are living in a society where everyone wants to do what is right in their own eyes. (God warns about this in Isaiah 5:20-21). Those who state that moral behavior should be defined by God's Word are labeled as intolerant and hateful. Isn't this called shooting the messenger?

Today, everyone seems to have their own opinion about what is moral. Somehow we have convinced ourselves that we have the right to do whatever we want. One of my former business associates considered himself to be a very moral person, always proud that he was doing the right thing. Upon further analysis, it became clear that he was making up his own rules for morality and that he was always in compliance with them. In Judges 17:6, Israelite morality was described this way: "every man did that which was right in his own eyes". In other words, the Israelites had drifted away from God's laws and were making up their own rules. Americans are doing the same thing! Do you really think that we won't be punished for this at some point?

Certainly some of the things we watch on television and at the theater have changed opinions about what is acceptable. Things that used to be shocking are now commonplace. Here are some disturbing trends in our morality:

- Pornography is now accessible to every home that has an Internet connection. Pornographers have learned how to snare our children when they make honest mistakes in typing or searching for a web address.
- The concept of friends with benefits is sweeping college campuses. This is an arrangement between two people to have an ongoing sexual relationship without becoming emotionally involved or committed.
- Many teenagers have decided that certain sexual acts are not really sex.
- One-fourth of American female teenagers have a sexually transmitted infection according to a 2008 report by the Centers for Disease Control and Prevention ("CDC"). [13]
- The CDC reported that around 40 percent of all births in America in 2007 were to unwed mothers. In 1980, this number was around 20 percent. [14] In 2012, various news articles reported that over half of all births to those under 30 were to unwed mothers.
- Various studies show that 40 percent to 50 percent of all marriages in the U.S. end in divorce. Divorces plus births outside of marriage means that huge numbers of children are growing up without fathers in the home.

Perhaps you don't consider some of these things to be immoral. I believe that God has a different viewpoint. God made man and woman for each other, to be bonded in marriage for life, and to enjoy sex within the marriage relationship.

There are many more examples that prove that our morality as a country has declined. Why is this important? First of all, it is important because we will suffer the consequences of living in an immoral society. These changes in behavior will create long term issues for our country and us as individuals. Perhaps nothing will have a greater impact on our future than the breakdown of the traditional family structure. Second, our behavior is contrary to God's Word and what he desires for us. Increased immorality is just an outward sign that we are moving away from God. The United States has been blessed by God beyond measure. Is it reasonable for us to expect that God will continue to bless us as a nation as we continue to move away from him? If you read the Bible, you will find that God severely punished the Israelites when they moved away from him. Our best days as a country may be behind us. Frankly, I find this depressing, and I think it is time to reverse the trend of moving away from God. We each need to do our part!

The Search for Spirituality

I chuckle sometimes when people say they are trying to find themselves. How hard could it be to find yourself? What they really mean is they are trying to figure out what type of person they are. This search often involves analyzing their spirituality.

There seems to be a huge interest in spirituality in America. We live in the richest, most prosperous country on Earth. The majority of our citizens live comfortably and do not have to suffer from some of the famines, wars, and poverty that we see in other parts of the world. Yet, it seems that everyone is still looking for something else. Perhaps we have learned that material things don't make us happy for very long. So, how are people trying to meet their spiritual needs?

One place that people seem to be looking is books. It is difficult to get exact figures for book sales, so I have averaged around five different sources (in 2009) which you can find on the Internet. The Bible is the best-selling book of all time, having sold 5 or 6 billion copies. The second best-selling book is *Quotations from Chairman Mao*, which is not surprising considering that China is the most populated country on Earth. Third is the Qur'an (sometimes referred to in English as the Koran), also not surprising in view of the fact that there are over one billion Muslims in the world.

The rest of the top ten list is fascinating. It includes two Harry Potter books plus *Lord of the Rings* and *The Da Vinci Code*. *The Da Vinci Code* sold around 65 million copies according to many estimates (including 45 million in the U.S.) and brought in another $750 million or so from the movie of the same name. This story is fictional and deals with the alleged marriage of Jesus Christ to Mary Magdalene and the cover-up that ensued to keep this out of our current religious beliefs. This book was wildly successful in the United States, where three-fourths of the citizens claim to be Christians. It is reasonable to assume that Christians made up a huge number of the readers and moviegoers. Why was this book such a huge success? I understand that most people like a good mystery or a scandal and are intrigued by cover-ups, but there are plenty of other mysteries that we can read that would be entertaining.

What makes *The Da Vinci Code* unique is that it is a fictional story about the life of Jesus. People did not read this book to find out who Jesus was – we can get all the information we need in the Bible. I think people read this book because they had a basic curiosity or skepticism, especially about spirituality, that needed to be satisfied. Perhaps many readers had doubts about whether the Bible's account of Jesus is true.

Our skeptical human nature gives many of us problems with religious beliefs. Many people cannot accept a key principle of Christianity, which is that faith in Jesus alone can save us rather than good works. This concept is just too good to be true for some people. Many people who have adopted Christianity are still skeptical about some of the things in the Bible. There are many things in the Bible that defy some of the laws of nature that we understand, but Jesus explains God's capabilities in Mark 10:27: "With man this is impossible, but not with God; all things are possible with God." This is a *very* important statement for us to believe!

Our search for spirituality reflects that we are often looking for things that we want to believe or we are looking for things that justify what we already believe. According to a survey taken by the Barna Group regarding *The Da Vinci Code*, only about 5 percent of all adults in the U.S. who read the book said that they changed any of their religious beliefs because of the book's content. [15] This sounds good initially, but it means that around 2 million Americans changed their religious beliefs after reading a completely fictional account about Jesus. Based on the survey sample, we can also infer that 11 million Americans would say that the book was helpful in relation to their personal spiritual growth or understanding. Does it make sense that this many people could change their religious beliefs by reading a non-religious book? Are these people attending a church regularly?

There are other books that people are reading to find spiritual answers. One is the book *God Is Not Great* by atheist Christopher Hitchens. This book was on the New York Times best seller list in the summer of 2007 and showed up again in early 2012 after Mr. Hitchens' death. This book criticizes almost everything that could be considered religious. Another example is Eckhart Tolle's book *A New Earth: Awakening To Your Life's Purpose*, a book containing many New Age concepts, which in 2008 became the fastest-selling book in the history of Borders bookstore due in large part to Oprah Winfrey's selection of it for her book club.

Why are books that are contrary to the Bible so popular? Why are so-called Christians reading these books? Are people looking for the truth or are they looking for things they want to believe that make them comfortable?

Interest in the Paranormal

It is not within the scope of this book to study paranormal events and beliefs in detail, but we need to look at their impact on religious beliefs. Is it coincidental that interest in spirituality is increasing at the same time as increased interest in the paranormal? There has always been a fascination with the unknown and unexplained, in particular with the concept of UFOs and alien visitation to the earth. After all, God lives up there, so what else is up there?

The fascination with the unknown is very obvious when you look at the amount of money grossed by movies dealing with outer space. A recent listing of the top twenty five movies of all time included *Star Wars* (the original), *Star Wars Episode I*, *Star Wars Episode III*, *Independence Day*, and *E.T. the Extra-Terrestrial*. According to my rough calculations, the Star Wars series of films has taken in around $5 billion not counting merchandise sales, making it the most successful film series ever.

Let's look at what Americans believe about UFOs and aliens based on a variety of survey results:

- 72 percent believe in extraterrestrials ("ETs").
- 48 percent believe in UFOs.
- 80 million people think we have been visited by extraterrestrials.
- 20 percent believe that aliens have abducted humans.

What do these surveys tell us about Americans? First of all, there is no evidence at all that there is life on other planets, yet almost three-fourths of Americans believe that there is. The second notable thing is that less than half believe in UFOs in spite of the fact that this is the phenomenon that appears to have evidence. *I think we can conclude that what some people believe is not related to the evidence available.* The Bible contains a large amount of evidence, but there are still people who don't believe it is true!

There is a close link between fascination with extraterrestrials and spirituality. Many New Age concepts can be traced directly to statements that were supposedly made by extraterrestrials! In most cases, the ETs have not made these statements in person but rather through speaking to human minds the same way that good and evil spirits influence our thoughts. Are these ETs physical or spiritual, or even real? More on this later...

If you look at the people who have dedicated their lives to studying UFOs and ETs, you would find that many of them think that ETs are coming here to help us save the planet. Is this more wishful thinking or are the ETs representatives of evil? Many movies, books, and television shows have revolved around the struggle between good and evil. We are going to explore the spiritual good-versus-evil battle later. We will find that there is a striking similarity between the behavior of the alleged aliens and evil spirits.

Summary

What have we learned in this chapter?

- America is moving away from God. This creates an environment that is receptive to new ideas about God.
- Many people who call themselves Christians don't attend church regularly and don't have a personal relationship with Jesus.
- Most U.S. Christians believe that there are multiple ways to God, contrary to Jesus' statement in the Bible.
- Most people believe in heaven, but many don't know how to get there and don't seem to be too concerned about it.
- New theories about God have entered our society and have become accepted as truth.
- There has been a significant decline in morality in America during the time when people have been moving away from God.
- Morality has become an individual or governmental opinion rather than something we get from the Bible.
- People are more interested in spirituality than ever before, but many are not looking to God for answers.
- What many people believe is not based on the available evidence.

CHAPTER 2:

Factors Which Affect Beliefs

This chapter deals with human tendencies that influence *why* we believe what we believe. No offense to anyone personally, but we also need to talk about why we don't really know as much as we think we do. We will see that our current thought processes make it difficult for some people to accept Christianity, and that our minds often open doors for Satan to spread false ideas about God. Hopefully, you can use this information to analyze your own thought process.

Until we are adults, other people usually tell us what we can or can't do, make decisions for us, and tell us what to believe. Hopefully, our parents taught us how to make good decisions. Once we reach adulthood, we realize that we have to make lots of decisions ourselves and live with the consequences. We can ask for advice, research the issues, pray, consult the Bible, trust our feelings, listen to Oprah Winfrey or Dr. Phil, or do some combination of these things to make a decision. However, the decision is still our responsibility. This is especially true when deciding what we believe about God.

If you have had teenage children, you know that at some point they start distancing themselves from you. Maybe you can remember your own time as a teenager when you couldn't believe how old-fashioned and out of touch your parents were. Teenagers find that they would much rather spend time with their friends than with their parents. They may think that your opinions are antiquated and you are too restrictive. This occurs at a time when they are trying to establish their own identity. This same behavior happens with God. At some point in their lives, many people start to move away from him. Perhaps they think he is out of touch or no longer relevant for their life. Perhaps they think he is antiquated or too restrictive. Perhaps they think they know their own needs better than God does. In many cases, people think they can get along without him. Who changed – the individual or God?

Think about these questions as they apply to you:

- Why do you believe what you believe about God?
- What individuals or life experiences influenced your decision-making?
- What part of your education or personality influenced your decision-making?
- If you believe there are many ways to God, why do you believe this?
- Where are you getting the facts that are the basis for your opinions?
- Who do you trust when you need advice?

Take a few moments, and see if you can come up with the answers to these questions.

Scientists have been studying the decision-making process in humans and have recently found evidence that supports a predominant theory: most decision-making is based on emotional rather than logical factors. This is true regardless of whether you are left-brain oriented or right-brain oriented. When we make emotional decisions, it means we are deciding on choices that just feel right or make us feel good. Many of our daily decisions are designed to make us feel good. For women, sometimes a good shopping trip or some chocolate can really help your attitude. For men, maybe it is a big steak or tickets to your favorite sporting event. There is no reason to believe that decisions about religion would be made any differently from other decisions that we all make. Does this mean that people could be looking for religious beliefs that they *want* to believe because these beliefs make them feel better? This is not only happening, but it was predicted in the book of Timothy in the Bible: "For the time will come when men will not put up with sound doctrine. Instead, to suit their own desires, they will gather around them a great number of teachers to say what their itching ears want to hear." [1]

After making emotional decisions, people typically use analytical and reasoning skills based on their knowledge and common sense to justify what they want to believe. Our human nature causes us to want to feel that the decisions we make are correct. Unfortunately, we don't always realize that our perspective and knowledge is limited – which in turn affects our decision making. And more importantly, just because a decision *feels* correct doesn't mean it actually *is* correct.

A common phrase is to *think outside the box*. To some extent, we are all in a box. The box is defined by the personalities we were born with, the educations we received, experiences we have had, our understanding of science and technology, and the capabilities of our minds. We are limited overall by the senses of sight, hearing, smell, taste and feel (each of which has individual limitations). We are constrained by the dimensions that we understand – space (length, width, and height) and time. And finally, we are limited by our own egos and our pride. This is the part of our brains that tells us that something cannot exist unless it fits within the limits of what we understand and experience. It is important that we deal with these limitations to help us fully understand God. We can never fully get out of the box, but we can expand the size of it. We never learn unless our boxes are expanding.

Our Increasing Self-Reliance

In the introduction to this book, I referred to *The Frog in the Kettle*. This book correctly predicted a number of changes that would occur in human thought processes, preferences, and behavior along with the effects that these changes would have on the religious environment in America. In this section, we will focus on the portions of that book that deal with self-reliance and how our preferences for self-reliance are changing religious beliefs.

The first points I would like to deal with are that people have become more selfish with their time and more specific with their desires. When I was in the workplace, I noticed that many younger workers were placing more emphasis on their benefits, including paid time off, than they were on how to improve their salaries or advance in the business. I also observed many of these workers planning their time off activities during working hours, with a focus on eliminating wasted time. Our younger generation has sometimes been labeled as the now generation – they want things now and they have very specific wants. Our enterprising businesses have done a good job of giving these people exactly what they want without forcing them to wait. Burger King's *have it your way* slogan was a good early example of this. More recently, the technology companies have fed the desire for instant information by combining telephone, texting, Internet access, social networking and more into a single handheld device. Perhaps you are even reading this book on one of these devices. Because many of our businesses are good at monitoring trends in the marketplace, they have done a good job of satisfying the desire for instant gratification. Many of us in the older age groups have happily followed along with these trends.

I can certainly relate to people who want to maximize their time and not waste any of it. As George Barna indicated in *The Frog in the Kettle*, people are not going to spend an hour or more in a church service if they do not feel that the service is a beneficial use of their time. Perhaps this is a factor in the decline in church attendance in the U.S. However, I think a bigger issue is the one caused by people's specific desires – i.e. the desire to get exactly what they want. I could understand someone leaving a church because they consider it a waste of their time, but would they abandon God completely because they consider him to be a waste of their time? Perhaps the real problem is that people are moving away from God because God is not telling them what they want to hear.

Our society has validated that it is acceptable for us to get exactly what we want by creating many choices. For example, when I was growing up we only had one TV (with a black and white picture) with three TV networks, and we were happy with our choices. Today, there are multiple TVs in our houses with hundreds of cable channels, and we still complain sometimes that we can't find anything worth watching. (There is a lot of truth in that statement). In addition, we now have Digital Video Recorders (DVRs) that enable us to record our favorite shows, watch them when we want to, and avoid wasting time watching commercials.

The trend of having multiple choices is now reflected in the practice of cafeteria religion, where a person chooses what they want to believe from either Christianity or other religions (or all of these). The result is a completely personalized religion designed by the individual which is, by definition, a religion that the individual is comfortable with. The problem with this approach is that the Bible is not a test with multiple choice or true/false answers. God doesn't tell us to pick three out of five things to believe. Likewise, he did not include in the Bible statements about himself or Jesus that are false. Are you a person who is uncomfortable with some of the things in the Bible, and you have chosen to ignore them or not believe them? Does this mean that these things are not true, or does it mean that you don't *want* to believe them?

We know that the practice of cafeteria religion is widespread today because of the statistics that show that the majority of people who call themselves Christians do not believe that Jesus is the only way to God. Since the Bible contains a direct statement by Jesus making it clear that he is the only way to God, we can safely say that the majority of Christians today are actually practicing cafeteria religion. If you believe that there are multiple ways to God, wake up! If you are practicing cafeteria religion, you are calling God a liar. This doesn't sound like a very comfortable religion to me. Are you allowing society's focus on political correctness to affect your belief in God's Word? Are you traveling the road to Jesus or the path of least resistance? Think about it!

Another trend we should discuss is that people have become more reliant on themselves. This may be related to a decrease in trust for others. Many of us have been disappointed in the past by employers, loved ones, our government officials, and even religious leaders. Several years ago, we tended to trust people in certain positions, but now this trust must be earned. The skepticism that we have developed may be appropriate based on what we have experienced in recent years.

Self-reliance causes a natural aversion to other people telling us what to do. We see this in children when they become two or three years old. Also, we think we know ourselves better than anyone else does. Therefore, there is a reluctance to allow other people to tell us what is good for us. This certainly applies to religion. Our churches have a reputation of telling people what they should believe, but our natural tendencies are to gather the facts and decide what to believe on our own. Our natural tendencies make cafeteria religion appealing since it allows us to make our own decisions about what to believe.

For many people, especially young people, we cannot ignore the effects of peer pressure. Peer pressure basically results in a person taking actions to avoid being ridiculed or being different than friends and associates. In other words, a person is concerned about what other people think about them. If you are like this, then there are two things you should know. First of all, other people aren't really thinking about you that much. Second, what God thinks about you is much more important than what your friends think. Have you really thought about the consequences of ignoring God's Word to please yourself or your friends and associates?

A number of well publicized scandals involving religious leaders have certainly not helped the image of Christianity in America. However, the real problem is not with the church organizations but the people who claim to be Christians. If you don't trust anyone and don't want other people telling you what to believe, you will not be happy in *any* church. In fact, you will not be happy with God either, because God requires that you trust him and believe him. The unique Christian concept of faith is based on trusting in God. Let me ask you some important questions. Do you have issues with organized religion or do you have issues with God? Can you honestly say that God has done something to cause you not to believe him or trust him? Do you have hard evidence that contradicts anything in the Bible?

The danger of self-reliance, or autonomy, is that it makes a person into his or her own god. The reason that the individual becomes their own god is that they make up their own version of the truth and are accountable only to themselves. In other words, there is a failure to submit to God. By not submitting to God, we become Christians in name only. We are not really opposed to God, but we are not really dedicated to him either. Jesus clearly states his dislike of "lukewarm" believers: "I know your deeds, that you are neither cold nor hot. I wish you were either one or the other! So, because you are lukewarm—neither hot nor cold—I am about to spit you out of my mouth." [2] Jesus is telling us that we make him sick when we are just Christians in name only!

Perhaps if we were all honest with ourselves, we would admit that self-reliance just masks some of our fears. We may find it difficult to place our trust in others because we don't want to be disappointed or hurt. We may find it difficult to turn our lives over to God because we are afraid of what he will do with them. We might want to rely on ourselves because that is the best way to get exactly what we want, regardless of whether we are getting what is best for us. Many people have convinced themselves that no one else can possibly know what is best for them. These things all reflect a lack of faith in God. Reliance on self is a sin because it separates us from God. We need to ask him to forgive us and help us overcome our weaknesses.

Our attempts to define our own religion basically end up with us trying to fit God into some sort of box that we have defined. The problem with this is that God is too big for a box!

We Don't Know As Much As We Think We Do

The Unknown

I had a boss a few years ago who mentally challenged me as much as anyone I have ever worked with. Frankly, I enjoyed this because it helped me learn and helped remind me that there are lots of things that I just don't know much about. One of my boss's favorite sayings was "you don't know what you don't know." This is one of those sayings that you need to read two or three times when thinking about what it means.

Perhaps I can explain this saying in this manner. There are some things out there that I don't know much about, and I realize that I don't know much about them. For example, one of my friends is a nuclear physicist. When he starts talking about nuclear technology, I get lost really quickly. Nuclear technology is something that I *know* that I don't know much about. On the other hand, there are subjects that I don't know anything about, and no one even knows what those subjects are. In the 1800s, nuclear physics didn't exist. There were no courses available because no one knew that nuclear physics existed or ever would exist. Even though we have made huge advances in our scientific knowledge in the last hundred years, it would be very naïve of us to assume that we have a good grasp on what it is that we don't know. We must admit that there is a large body of information called the unknown. Admitting that we don't know as much as we think we do is a key in allowing us to obtain a better understanding of God. Having faith to accept things that just don't fit into your box of knowledge is a necessary step in understanding the power and majesty of God. The apostle Paul referred to the problem of seeing the unknown when he referred to the fact that we cannot see everything clearly while we are on Earth but that everything will be revealed to us when we get to heaven: "Now we see but a poor reflection as in a mirror; then we shall see face to face. Now I know in part; then I shall know fully, even as I am fully known." [3]

In my first job after college, one of the senior managers in the company gave me some great advice, which I have never forgotten. It was: "you will not be successful in this company until you realize how much that you don't know." I had been under the impression that college would teach me most of what I needed to know. Once I realized that I had a lot to learn, I became eager to learn, and my knowledge box expanded considerably.

Here is an example of how the box we are in limits our thinking. NASA recently sent a space vehicle to Mars to collect samples and analyze the environment. One of the stated purposes is to see if there was or is water on Mars and whether the planet could have supported life at some point. Are we looking for life as it is defined by the scientific knowledge that we have (the box we are in)? We are assuming that water, oxygen, and certain basic elements that we have on Earth are required for life. Why not allow for the possibility that life could exist in other forms? For example, what if an animal could live by breathing carbon dioxide instead of oxygen? The fact that we have put constraints on what we are looking for could cause us to not see what is actually there! This is an analogy that certainly applies to religion!

Another problem with our knowledge boxes is that each of us has a different perspective, and our perspectives are limited. Because of this, two people can look at the same thing and interpret it differently. Our beliefs about God will most likely be influenced by our perspectives.

We need to realize that our quest for knowledge is simply that we are trying to learn what God already knows. If you take God's knowledge minus our knowledge, the difference equals the unknown that each of us faces. How big is the box of knowledge that you understand compared to the box containing the unknown? Surely the contents of the unknown box have shrunk in the during your lifetime, but how much is remaining? The point could be made that "we just don't know what we don't know."

Many atheists say that God doesn't exist because we can't prove that he does exist. (Of course, the atheists cannot prove that he *doesn't* exist). Let me rephrase what the atheists believe by using the box analogy: "God doesn't exist because there is nothing in my knowledge box that could explain him." This is the same as saying that there is nothing in the unknown box of knowledge. To deny that there are still things we don't know or understand just doesn't make sense. Likewise, saying that something doesn't exist just because we can't prove it using our limited knowledge doesn't pass the common sense test.

Pride

In the previous section we discussed the fact that we don't realize how much we don't know. In this section, we will deal with our attitudes about what we *do* know. For those of you who have attended college, I will bet that you didn't get through your first year without at least one professor telling you that there is no God. Various studies have shown that the more intelligent a person is, the less likely he or she is to believe in God. Approximately half of all professors say that they are strong believers in God (compared to three-fourths of the U.S. population).[4] So, why have many of our supposedly smartest citizens thought their way out of believing in God? Is it because they are smarter than the rest of us, and we just haven't figured it out yet? On the contrary, a person who figures out that there is no God can't possibly be called smart. This shows a total disregard for the evidence that exists. Perhaps pride is the largest single factor that causes smart, highly educated people to deny God's existence.

There is no question that the information we have acquired has exploded in the last hundred years or so. The problem with all of this knowledge is that we tend to become proud of what we know. Humans are clearly the most advanced form of being on Earth. As a society, we don't see many limits to what we can do. We have perfected cloning, cured many diseases, invented computers that are incredibly fast, discovered DNA and how to use it, and harnessed atomic energy. We invented microwave ovens, computers, cell phones, airplanes, automobiles, television, and many other modern devices. However, these accomplishments may lead us to believe that we are smarter than we really are.

Since our inventions are really just discoveries of things that God already knew about, then why should we feel pride in discovering something that God already knew? Instead, we should be amazed at God's creations. These things have been revealed to us according to his plan. For many people, more knowledge has a negative effect. The more they know, the smarter they think they are, the prouder they become, and the less they feel a need to rely on God.

A good example of the misuse of pride is in the term *self-made man*. I can appreciate people who start with very little and work their way into being successful. But, are we supposed to believe that God didn't bless them with any skills, intelligence, or abilities? Are we to believe that no one ever helped them along the way?

If we develop pride, pride can restrict our ability to learn. It becomes difficult to admit that we don't know it all! Many people want to think that they are as smart as God - that they are smart enough to figure out things on their own without relying on him.

The Bible has a lot to say about pride. Satan was an angel who rebelled against God. He was one of God's best creations, but he decided that he should be equal to God. He didn't like playing second fiddle! In Ezekiel 28:17, God tells us why Satan rebelled: "Your [Satan's] heart became proud on account of your beauty, and you corrupted your wisdom because of your splendor". His pride was what drove him to rebel against God, and this is what continues to motivate him to try to pull us away from God. Satan's pride has caused him to think that he can actually be equal to God. When we let our pride control how we think, we are emulating Satan. When you accomplish something, do you brag on yourself or give credit to God?

Psalms 10:4 says: "In his pride the wicked does not seek him; in all his thoughts there is no room for God." This verse reminds us that a prideful man will not seek God because a prideful man believes that he can control his life better on his own. There are quite a few people like this today. What they want for themselves is more important than anything God would want to give them. Perhaps you know people like this.

Here are some additional quotes from the Bible about pride:

> "When pride comes, then comes disgrace, but with humility comes wisdom." [5]

> "Pride only breeds quarrels, but wisdom is found in those who take advice." [6]

> "Pride goes before destruction, a haughty spirit before a fall." [7]

> "You say, 'I am rich; I have acquired wealth and do not need a thing.' But you do not realize that you are wretched, pitiful, poor, blind and naked." [8]

Notice that two of these verses refer to wisdom. Wisdom is how we apply and utilize our knowledge and realizing that we don't know as much as we think we do. Obtaining wisdom from God helps us discern the truth. We can humble ourselves before God and allow him to reveal things we had not previously understood. This requires that we swallow our pride.

In 1 Corinthians 1:25, Paul reminds us of this: "For the foolishness of God is wiser than a man's wisdom and the weakness of God is stronger than man's strength." Thinking that we are as wise as God is one of the most foolish mistakes that we could make. Thinking that we don't need to rely on God because we can handle things ourselves may indicate that we have pride that is getting in the way of the truth. Can you think of any examples where your decisions have been influenced by pride?

Faith

There is an old story that defines faith better than trying to explain it. A group of people were watching Charles Blondin walk across Niagara Falls on a tightrope while pushing a wheelbarrow. He had crossed many other times using various other props. Someone yelled out that they believed he could cross with a man in the wheelbarrow. Mr. Blondin invited the spectator to sit in the wheelbarrow, but he declined. The spectator believed that it could be done, but not enough to put his life in danger. Faith means that you trust someone completely!

Faith is a core concept of Christianity. What makes Christianity unique among world religions is that you can obtain eternal life with God by faith alone. All other religions that believe in a god rely on rules and/or good works to obtain God's blessings. Faith means accepting that God exists even though you can't see him. It means believing that Jesus is his Son because God said he was. It means believing that Jesus will provide his believers with eternal life because he said he would. Faith means that you don't need to prove that these things are true because you believe that God defines what is true and that "it is impossible for God to lie". [9]

Why do so many people have so much trouble with the concept of faith? There are a number of reasons. First, we tend to be skeptical, especially involving things that we can't see or touch. My generation was responsible for some of this attitude. One of our mottos in the 1960s was "don't trust anyone over thirty", and we just kept changing the age limit as we got older. Over time, this motto has just morphed into "don't trust anyone."

We may also feel that Jesus is just too good to be true. Why would Jesus die for us and give us eternal life? Why can we be saved simply by believing? Many people believe in the saying "there is no such thing as a free lunch" because everything comes with a price. Religions that are based on good works appeal to our human nature. Christianity, however, is based on the fact that Jesus, the sinless Son of God, paid the price for our sins by dying on a cross on our behalves. Our salvation comes from Jesus, and all we have to do to obtain it is believe in him. This may not be logical, but it is true! Good works will please God, but they will not provide salvation. Believing in Jesus with all of our heart is the faith that God is expecting from us.

Perhaps some of our skepticism also comes from the fact that we have been "burned" a few times. We may have been let down by friends, family, co-workers, and others. This makes us a little more cautious. The good news is that God will not disappoint us. This doesn't mean that God will give us all of our selfish desires. But, it does mean that he will deliver the promises that he makes to us in the Bible.

Another problem that people have with faith is that many events in the Bible don't seem logical. Miracles like the virgin birth, the resurrection, healing the sick, raising the dead, and walking on water just don't fit into our boxes of knowledge. They can't be explained logically or scientifically, and therefore it is difficult to believe them. Not believing that these events occurred reveals small thinking by us. Just because we can't explain these things doesn't mean that God can't do them. As we saw earlier, Jesus reminds us that there are no limitations with God in Mark 10:27: "With man this is impossible, but not with God; all things are possible with God." Your faith will be strengthened when you accept the fact that *all* things are possible with God.

Faith means believing in things we can't see, as explained in Hebrews 11:1: "Now faith is being sure of what we hope for and certain of what we do not see." Our human nature causes us to want to see something or be able to prove its existence before we can believe that it is real. We can't see God, but God sent his Son Jesus to help us see him. Jesus said "Anyone who has seen me has seen the Father." [10]

Let me give you a simple example of faith. Think about the last time you flew on an airplane. Did you know the pilot personally? Are you sure that he had the proper education and experience to fly you to your destination? Did you know all the workers who inspected and serviced the plane? Did you verify that they did their jobs correctly and didn't make any mistakes? I could go on and on, but the point is simple. You turned your life over to these people. You could be killed if any one of them made a critical mistake. Yet, you were willing to take this risk. There is no risk in having faith in Jesus! In fact, the risk to you is much greater if you don't have faith in Jesus. If you reject or ignore Jesus, you will spend eternity separated from God. I will explain what this really means later in this book.

Faith is a difficult concept for many to accept because it is so simple. We need to ask God to help us overcome our human weaknesses that prevent us from believing God's Word.

The Spirit World

Certainly one of the things that we don't fully understand is the spirit world. Jesus says that "God is a spirit, and his worshippers must worship in spirit and in truth." [11] What does it really mean to say that God is a spirit? What is a spirit anyway?

In the Greek version of John's gospel, the word used for spirit actually means "breath" or "wind." There are some interesting analogies in comparing spirit to the wind. The wind cannot be seen but it can be heard. You really don't know where it is coming from or where it is going. In fact, it seems to go wherever it wants, and it is not always in the same direction. Wind can be very powerful and destructive or very pleasant. Wind has been around for a long time and will be here forever.

Each of us consists of a physical body, a mind, and a spirit. Your mind links your spirit to your physical body. The Bible tells us that God made man in his own image, but obviously there are differences between our physical bodies and the Spirit of God because our physical bodies will *all* die at some point. I believe that we are like God in the ways that we think and feel. So, we are not spirits but we have a spiritual nature. Our spiritual nature changes when we accept Jesus as our Savior because God sends his Holy Spirit to live within us.

Here are some things that we know about the spirit world: God, Jesus, and his angels live in heaven. The Bible describes heaven as a place where each Christian will live in his spiritual body after he dies. The Bible tells us that our physical bodies will be transformed into spiritual bodies, similar to how Jesus was transformed after his resurrection.

Satan was an angel (a spirit) who rebelled against God in spite of his lofty position in heaven. Satan and the evil spirits who joined his rebellion are roaming the earth creating havoc and temptation for us. Satan's agenda is to replace God. As part of his plan, he creates doubts in our minds about things that are clear in the Bible. These doubts are designed to pull us away from God. Don't forget this as you make decisions on a daily basis!

So, we know that there are good and evil spirits out there somewhere who are trying to influence us. But, we don't know too much about how they operate and how they are able to defy some of the laws of science and nature that we understand. For example, these spirits can become physical and then disappear. They can defy gravity. And, they don't seem to be bound by our space and time dimensions. These spirits seem to be living in a dimension that we don't understand.

Scientifically, we have not really proven what a spirit is. Is a spirit some sort of light or energy mass? We just don't know, and it doesn't really matter. Will further scientific discoveries help us believe in the spirit world, or will we use these discoveries to explain them as natural phenomena instead of creations of God? The Bible tells us that those who do not have the Holy Spirit living in them will not understand the mysteries of the spirit world: "The man without the Spirit does not accept the things that come from the Spirit of God, for they are foolishness to him, and he cannot understand them, because they are spiritually discerned." [12] We can infer from this passage that having the Holy Spirit in us will greatly help our understanding of the spirit world.

Because we have a spiritual nature, we realize that there is more going on than what our five senses can detect. We realize that there is something else that makes us complete. Do you believe that your spirit was created by God? God says that he knew you before you were born: "Before I formed you in the womb I knew you, before you were born I set you apart." [13] God says that your spirit returns to him when we die: "and the dust returns to the ground it came from, and the spirit returns to God who gave it." [14] These verses confirm that God gave each of you your spirit and it returns to him upon your death. However, this doesn't mean that we all end up in heaven.

We need to admit that there is still much about the spiritual world that we just don't fully understand. We need to avoid relying on our own understanding instead of the understanding we can obtain through the Holy Spirit.

Deciding We Are Smarter Than God

Earlier, we talked about things that sometimes prevent us from seeing or accepting the truth. Some of these things lead us to start thinking that we are smarter than God. How could someone think they are smarter than God since God knows everything? This is pride at its worst. Nonetheless, there are a number of intellectuals who think they have God figured out and can explain away many of the things that are clear in the Bible. What I don't understand is how people can read a book by one of these intellectuals and then decide to believe what they are reading. The authors of these books are not bringing messages *from* God, but *about* God. Wouldn't it make more sense to listen to and learn from God directly?

Another phenomenon we are seeing in our society is what I call *celebrity disease.* This often occurs when a person becomes famous, successful, or wealthy. Celebrity disease is a disease of the ego. People with celebrity disease decide that they are better than everyone else because they are famous and/or rich. People in the media help encourage this disease. At some point, many of these people decide they don't need God or they can redefine God in some way. In 2007, one of our wealthiest movie stars (who grew up in a Baptist church) announced that he didn't need God anymore because he felt that he could handle things better himself. What do you think God's opinion of people like this is? Jesus said "Indeed, it is easier for a camel to go through the eye of a needle than for a rich man to enter the kingdom of God." [15] Even people who are not rich or famous have adopted the belief that they don't really need God because they can handle things better on their own. The problem with this belief is that God owns everything we have, and he can take it away at any time. We are fooling ourselves if we think we have control over our lives and our possessions. If you didn't learn that during the most recent recession, then you weren't really paying attention.

King Solomon was one of the wisest men who ever lived. He asked God for wisdom and received it, but he was still not wiser than God. In Ecclesiastes 1:9, Solomon said "What has been will be again, what has been done will be done again; there is nothing new under the sun." Perhaps you have heard the saying "there is nothing new under the sun" previously. Now you know where it came from. There is some timeless wisdom in this statement, as you will see below.

In the first century A.D., there was a group of people known as Gnostics. Recent discoveries have revealed some of their texts, including the gospel of Thomas. Skeptics are wondering why some of these early writings were not included in the Bible, but the fact is that they were written much later than the biblical gospels at a time when no eyewitnesses to Jesus were available. The word Gnostic came from a Greek word that meant knowledge. These people were early intellectuals! Gnostics believed that salvation from sin and evil came through secret knowledge. Many of them believed that Jesus was a revealer who came to reveal the secrets of the spiritual world to a select few and to lead them to find the divine identity deep within. In other words, they thought that your mind could lead you to a higher level of consciousness. Gnostics tended to view key events in the Bible as symbolic events only, rather than things that actually happened. Gnostic thoughts still exist in our modern society.

Statistics show that interest in spirituality is increasing and interest in organized religion is decreasing. Gnosticism is appealing today to people who are looking for divinity within, who want to find divinity on their own rather than through a structured religion, and who just can't accept the Bible as being true. Satan is smart enough to know that our society has become more self-centered, and he is convincing people that they can invent their own religion. (There is nothing new under the sun). Intellectualism still won't help us find God, but it can lead us down the path of thinking that we are smarter than God or equal to him. God gives us a specific warning about this: "Trust in the LORD with all your heart and lean not on your own understanding; in all your ways acknowledge him, and he will make your paths straight." [16] Trusting in God is not an intellectual exercise that requires each person to rely on his own intelligence. In fact, God told us specifically to not lean on our own understanding. Instead, God tells us to lean on him for the understanding that we need.

A popular belief today is that God just wouldn't exclude anyone from heaven. But, this is not the truth. We may not think God is fair, but God *is* fair. He gives everyone an equal chance to accept him or reject him. We need to realize that God makes the rules and he will bless who he chooses. God said to Moses: "I will have mercy on whom I have mercy, and I will have compassion on whom I have compassion." [17] It is not our purpose to try to outsmart God, but rather to trust in what he says to us in the Bible.

Do you know people who have decided that they don't need God because things are going so well for them? Do you know people who feel that they can handle any situation and don't need God's assistance? Have you ever thought this way?

When Seeing Is Not Believing

You have probably heard the phrase "seeing is believing" all of your life. In most cases, this saying proves to be true. How many times have you said "I need to see that for myself"? This usually refers to something that is outside what you consider normal or expected, and you really can't believe it unless you see it. One of the objections to a faith-based religion like Christianity is that some people will say they can't believe unless they can see evidence. These people are failing to acknowledge that the Bible contains evidence written down by eyewitnesses.

Sometimes seeing is not believing! For example, there were thousands of people who saw Jesus, heard him speak, and witnessed the miracles, yet some still did not believe. The Jewish leaders who followed him around because they were threatened by him did not believe, even though Jesus fulfilled hundreds of Old Testament prophecies. How could this be? The answer is very simple. Jesus was not what they were looking for or what they wanted. They were looking for a messiah made in their own image. We talked about the danger of looking for something specific earlier in this chapter - it can cause you to miss the things that are right in front of you.

I had an embarrassing experience right after I got married. I was working on an out-of-town client engagement. My wife had decided to go with me since we were traveling to my hometown. I had worked for a couple of years before I got married, and I was not used to having my wife around during an out-of-town assignment. One day, I was walking back into my client's office after having gone out to lunch with some of my associates. As I went through the reception area, I noticed two women sitting off to my left side. I acknowledged them, smiled, and kept on walking. I remember thinking that one of them was about my age and very nice-looking. Then I heard a voice call out my name. About that time it hit me. That was my wife and my mother sitting in the reception area! I had looked right at them and not realized who they were! (This is not a good way to start a marriage).

What happened? Well, I was out of town and not expecting to see anyone that I knew. Not only that, neither my mother nor my wife had ever driven to a client's office to see me. Finally, my wife had been shopping and was wearing a short hair wig. I had never seen her with anything but long hair, and it really did change her looks. (At least that was the excuse I used). The point is that my mind was convinced that I would not see them, and therefore I didn't.

Sometimes we just don't see things that are right in front of us. Does that mean that those things are not there? No, it just means that we didn't see them.

Our bodies have physical limitations also. The colors we see are based on the light waves emitted from each object. However, there are light waves that we can't see. Ultraviolet light and infrared light are outside that range of light waves that our eyes and minds can interpret. If you have ever been sunburned, you know that ultraviolet light exists even though you can't see it. Similar analogies apply to our other senses (hearing, smell, touch, and taste). We know that many animals have capabilities in these areas that are not available to us as humans.

I am sure you realize that there are radio and TV signals in the airwaves no matter where you are. You can't hear them or see them without the assistance of a radio or television. The reason is that the frequencies are outside the capabilities of our sight and hearing senses. Likewise, there are spirits among us right now that we can't see or hear. We shouldn't assume that something doesn't exist unless we can see or hear it.

The Bible is the written Word in which God reveals himself to us. The Holy Spirit is provided by God to help us understand spiritual matters. The human mind is not able to comprehend these things without assistance from God. Is your search for spirituality missing the mark because you are looking for the wrong things in the wrong places? Is the Holy Spirit living within you to help you understand these spiritual matters? Have you asked God to help you get a better understanding of his Word?

Our Perspective and Personality

Sometimes a scientist will see something that will be rejected by a religious person. Sometimes, just the opposite occurs. Science and religion haven't always mixed well. Think about this: if you have people from twenty different professions look at something, they may all see something different. Put a person in front of an elephant and another behind the elephant, and then ask them what they see. Everyone's perspective is different. We need to remind ourselves that the complete picture is often the sum of what everyone saw.

We all have different abilities and personalities that affect our viewpoints. When looking at information, the complete picture is usually obtained by collecting all of the information from all of the viewpoints. We can't just look at most things from one point of view and assume that our viewpoints reveal everything we need to know. Only God is able to do this. Is it possible that you have failed to recognize some of the truths in the Bible because your own viewpoint keeps you from being open minded enough to accept God's truth?

Accordingly, it doesn't make sense to take one person's opinion about God and decide to believe it blindly. This is especially true because of the lies being spread by Satan to confuse us and pull us away from God. We need to test these statements against the Bible itself to look for inconsistencies. If we read or hear something that is directly contrary to the Bible, then what we read or heard is not from God!

For many people, perceptions become realities. In other words, you can convince yourself that whatever you believe is the truth. In fact, if you didn't think something was true, then you wouldn't believe it! I used to work with a guy who was the king of false truths. He would make a statement during a meeting that was a statement of opinion rather than a statement of fact. Then, he would treat his original statement as being fact and base all of his other arguments on his original statement. Most people would get caught up in the additional arguments (which sounded logical) and not stop to think that the basis for his entire set of arguments was not factual. (Sounds like some of our modern day politicians!) Today, we see this same thing going on in print media, Internet chat rooms and message boards. When it comes to Christianity, there is an underlying truth! We should not treat the perceptions that some people have about God as truth unless they are consistent with the Bible.

Do you realize that much of what you hear and read is actually propaganda? Do you believe that the national news channels are reporting all the news (just the facts), or do you believe that they are reporting what they want you to hear (along with their spin on what it means)? It seems that everyone has some sort of agenda today. How do you know what to believe?

I believe that many people are allowing someone other than God to tell them what to believe about God. In fact, many people are deciding what to believe about God without fully investigating the facts that are recorded in the Bible. Wouldn't it make more sense to get information directly from God? Wouldn't it make sense to remove barriers in the way we think to help us discern the truth? Wouldn't it make sense to actually look for the truth rather than just finding things we want to believe?

Summary

What have we learned in this chapter? Let's take a look.

- We tend to make decisions based on what makes us feel good.
- Our desires to get exactly what we want lead to inventing a comfortable religion.
- Self-reliance pulls us away from God and creates a false sense of confidence.
- Our perspectives are limited by our physical senses and existing knowledge.
- We don't know as much as we think we do.
- We aren't sure how big the unknown is.
- We don't fully understand the spiritual world.
- Pride affects our ability to learn and humble ourselves before God.

- Our human nature makes us skeptical of faith.
- We tend to dismiss things that we can't explain.
- We tend to see and hear what we want to.
- Our human weaknesses make many people receptive to false theories about God.

We need to deal with these issues to help us recognize the truth.

CHAPTER 3:

The Search for Truth

Millions of Americans have moved away from God in the last two decades, perhaps because they feel that God is not providing the answers they need, or they just don't like the answers they are getting. In the last chapter, we talked about factors that make it easier for us to be deceived.

Interest in spirituality seems to be at an all-time high. Yet, the search for spirituality is not necessarily a search for truth. As we discussed already, too many people are looking for something they *want* to believe rather than looking for the absolute truth. Are you one of these people? Are you a person who thinks there is no such thing as absolute truth? Perhaps this famous movie line applies to you: "you can't handle the truth". The first step in finding the truth is to be receptive to it. If we want to know the truth about God, then we have to be willing to listen to *everything* he says and not just parts of what he says.

In this chapter, we will talk about the predominant religions in the world and how they differ. We will also look at some of the new beliefs that are creeping into our society. While much of this material may be familiar, you may learn some things that will enlighten you. Hopefully, this analysis will help you see where your beliefs currently fit and how some of the new ideas simply can't be correct. But the most important point of this chapter will be to help you decide how to determine truth. One thing that all these religions have in common is that their followers think they are believing the truth.

We heard a lot about religion in 2012. First of all, a member of the Mormon church was the Republican nominee for President. Religion became a political issue because there is very little understanding about what Mormons actually believe. I remember a similar concern when John Kennedy was running for President in 1960. He was a Catholic, and people were concerned about the influence that the Pope might have over him. The Mormons have recently started a public relations campaign to try to alleviate some of the concerns about their religion.

The second thing that we heard a lot about in 2012 was "Tebowing". This, or course, is the act of kneeling in public and engaging in prayer or acknowledging God. Tim Tebow has made this famous on the football field, and it has polarized America. He has become both one of our most admired and most disliked athletes at the same time. Many people believe that there is no place for religion in a sporting event.

One trend we have seen in our society is relativism – the belief that what is true for you and what is true for me can be opposites and both will be true. This concept defies logic, and we are not going to spend much time on it. Closely related to relativism is the way people spin the truth to accomplish a specific purpose. Several years ago, I heard a speaker describing a U.S. versus Russia track meet that occurred during the Cold War era. He said that the U.S. won the meet. The Russian media reported the results by saying that the Russians had finished second and the U.S. finished next to last! Now, I don't know if this story is true, but it illustrates my point. This statement is factual but gives you a distorted view of what happened. We will see later how Satan is the master at coming up with distorted versions of the truth.

There are certain situations where it is acceptable for us to have different beliefs. For example, your definition of the ideal political candidate may differ from mine. However, each of us thinks our position is correct and true. These conflicting beliefs are appropriate because these are matters of opinion, and there is no absolute truth in this area. However, relativism does not work in matters related to God because there is an underlying *reality* that defines what is true. Either God exists, or he doesn't. If one person believes that God exists and another person doesn't, then one is right, and one is wrong. What each person believes has nothing to do with whether God actually exists. Relativism occurs when a person's opinions about a matter are viewed as truth rather than what they really are – opinions.

We are going to discuss the truth about God as an absolute concept. Perhaps you are a person who does not believe that God is a real being or that heaven and hell are real places. If so, you need to look at the evidence that is in this book.

When two conflicting religions have opposite views on something, how do we know which one is right? Where do we get the information we need to make a decision? How do we know whether information is coming from God or Satan? What does God say about how we should determine truth? Let's explore these questions.

Major Religions

The world's religions can be grouped into two categories – those that believe in a single all powerful god, and those that believe in either multiple gods or multiple ways to a single god (who may not be the same for everyone). The majority of people in the world are a member of one of these religious groups. Those who are non-religious include atheists (who believe that God does not exist) and those who just aren't sure what to believe or consider religion to be unimportant. Let's examine these groups briefly as part of identifying the truth about God.

Single, All Powerful God

Over half of the world's population believes in a single, all powerful God. The predominant religions in this group, listed in order of date established, are Judaism, Christianity, and Islam.

Judaism

The roots of Judaism go back to Abraham in approximately 2000 B.C. The Torah, duplicated in the first five books of the Christian Bible, records the history of God's interaction with Abraham and his descendants and records the laws given by God to Moses and the Israelites. Jews believe that God ("Jehovah") is a single being, eternal and omnipotent. They believe that God knows our thoughts and deeds and that he will punish or reward us accordingly. Judaism is primarily a religion of works and obeying God's laws. Most followers of Judaism are Jewish by birth, but this is not a requirement. Likewise, many people who are Jewish by birth are non-religious. Religious Jews do not believe that Jesus was the messiah promised by their religion but was a prophet who was the son of Joseph. They believe that Jesus died and was not resurrected. Jews believe that a messiah will be sent from God, but most Jews do not believe that the coming messiah will be the Son of God, because they believe that God exists in singular form and cannot have a son. Orthodox Jews believe in a resurrection of the righteous dead when their messiah comes during the end times, as stated in Daniel 12:2: "Multitudes who sleep in the dust of the earth will awake: some to everlasting life, others to shame and everlasting contempt."

Popular Jewish beliefs about their messiah are that he has not yet come, he will rebuild the temple in Jerusalem, he will promote peace and harmony among all nations, he will promote global acceptance of the Jewish religion and their God, and he will facilitate the return of Jews to Israel.

Christianity
Christianity began in approximately 33 A.D. after the death and resurrection of Jesus Christ. Christians believe that Jesus was the Son of God, born to the Virgin Mary with no earthly biological father. Jesus and most of the early Christians were Jewish, but the religion spread rapidly to non-Jewish believers. Christians worship the same God (Jehovah) as Jews and share many beliefs about God with Judaism. Jewish history and laws are included in the Christian Bible. Christians believe that Jesus was the Messiah promised in the Old Testament. He was sent because God realized that our imperfect sin nature would never allow us to measure up to his standards. By allowing Jesus to become a sacrifice on our behalf, each of us can have eternal life in heaven simply by believing that Jesus is the Son of God and trusting him as our Lord and Savior. This fact makes Christianity

unique among all religions. Eternal life is achieved based totally on who Jesus is, what he has done through his crucifixion and resurrection from the dead, and our accepting Jesus as our Savior rather than how well we followed a set of rules. Christians believe that Jesus was crucified, rose on the third day, and later ascended into heaven to be with God. Furthermore, Christians believe Jesus will return during the end times to retrieve his followers and deliver God's final judgment on the earth.

Christians also believe in the Trinity of God. This is the belief that God the Father, his Son Jesus, and the Holy Spirit are three persons but part of the same God. This is a very difficult concept to explain, and human analogies just aren't adequate. One way to understand this is that there are three views of the same God, in that he has revealed himself in three different ways. Christians believe in a single God (not three separate Gods).

Islam

Islam is the newest of these three religions. It was started by the prophet Muhammad in approximately 610A.D. Islam teaches that there is only one god (Allah) and that he revealed the text of the Qur'an to his prophet Muhammad through the angel Gabriel. According to tradition, Muhammad was carried on a journey to heaven where he met with Moses, Abraham, Jesus and other prophets who preceded him. Islam teaches that man is born sinless and remains that way unless he rebels against Allah. Islam also teaches that Jesus is a prophet rather than God's Son and that God did not have a son. Followers of Islam (Muslims) believe that Jesus did not die on the cross and rise again. Islam is a religion of works, meaning that you are judged when you die based on how you lived. This judgment determines whether you go to paradise or hell in the afterlife. The Qur'an provides guidelines on what is considered good behavior. Islam also supports the concept of the end times when Allah will judge both the dead and the living for the last time.

The differences between Jehovah and Allah can be confusing to many people. First of all, Islam acknowledges the prophets in Jewish history as recorded in the Old Testament. Islam treats both Jesus and Muhammad as great prophets who were sent by the Creator. Second, many of the Arab nations (which are predominantly Muslim) can trace their lineage to Abraham, whose grandson Jacob (renamed Israel by God) was the father of the twelve sons who fathered the twelve tribes of Israel (i.e. the Jewish nation). Some of the modern conflict between Arabs and Jews can be traced to events in the family of Abraham. Finally, the Qur'an includes versions of many events and stories in both Jewish and Christian tradition. These beliefs may cause people to believe that Jehovah and Allah are the same. However, revelations received by Muhammad are different than those given by God as recorded in the Bible. This fact alone means that Jehovah and Allah cannot be the same. The most important difference between Islam and Christianity is that Islam teaches that Jesus is *not* the Son of God and Christianity teaches that he *is* the Son of God.

Interestingly, Shiite Muslims believe that a messiah, whom they refer to as the Mahdi, will come during the end times. They believe that the Mahdi will return along with Jesus to rid the world of evil. We will look at more details about this belief, parallels with the Bible, and possible implications for us in the chapters on the end times.

All three of these religions are convinced that they are getting their information directly from God. However, there are significant differences in beliefs between these religions. Here are some of the most significant ones:

- Christians believe that Jesus is the Son of God. Jews and Muslims believe that their God did not have a son.
- Christians believe that Jesus died and was resurrected on the third day. Jews and Muslims do not believe that Jesus was resurrected.
- Christians believe that your place in the afterlife is secured based on belief in Jesus' atoning death rather than good works. Muslims and Jews say that your behavior is more important to their God.
- Christians believe that Jesus was the Messiah for whom the Jews have been waiting. Muslims and Jews say that Jesus was a prophet, not their messiah.

- Christians believe that the Jesus will return in the end times. Jews believe that a more earthly king or ruler will appear. Some Muslims believe that Jesus will come back as a prophet who will point to the Mahdi as their messiah.

The simple truth is that all three of these religions can't be correct! Either Jesus is the Son of God, or he isn't. Either faith in Jesus will get us to heaven, or it won't. Either Jesus was resurrected, or he wasn't. We just can't logically accept that opposite beliefs can both be correct. Does it make sense that God would say something to one group of people and then say something completely opposite to another group? God establishes truth, and it is absolute rather than relative. The reality is that God has given the same message to *everyone* through the Bible and his Son Jesus! Christians believe in this message, and the other religions have rejected it.

Since God establishes truth, then we need to look to God for the truth instead of looking somewhere else! In the next chapter, we will discuss how we know that the Bible contains truth. We need to pray that God will give us the wisdom to discern between all the conflicting definitions of what he expects from us.

No God or No Proof of God

Most people associate the term *atheist* with a person who believes that God does not exist. While this is true, atheism can take many forms. Some atheists who deny the existence of God may believe in other forms of spirituality, while others may deny the existence of any type of deity. Atheists tend to be skeptical of anything supernatural because the supernatural cannot be proved by the laws of nature or experienced by our body's senses. Strong atheists tend to go to great lengths explaining why God doesn't exist or coming up with alternate explanations for miracles and events in the Bible. Perhaps they do this to help convince themselves that they are right and because they realize the serious consequences of being wrong.

Most agnostics believe that it is impossible to obtain proof for God or spiritual matters; therefore they believe that there is no evidence one way or the other as to whether God exists. In other words, they believe that he might exist and he might not. Agnostics are slightly different than atheists, but both groups have rejected God. Jesus tells us why in Luke 11:23: "He who is not with me is against me". Unlike atheists, an agnostic may believe that there is a God even though there is no proof of God's existence. However, most agnostics tend to ignore God as either not existing or not being relevant, and they live their lives as though God does not exist. Many agnostics will admit that they can't prove that God *doesn't* exist, but they tend to ignore him anyway. As we learned in an earlier chapter, agnostics are growing in number at a significant rate.

Multiple Gods or Ways to God

The rest of the world's religious groups believe in multiple gods, multiple ways to a god, and various other definitions of deities. We will focus on Hinduism, Buddhism, and Chinese traditional spiritual practices since these have the largest number of followers and are the ones you are most likely to encounter.

Hinduism

There are over 900 million Hindus in the world, making this the world's third largest religion. More than 95 percent of Hindus live in India. Hinduism consists of a wide variety of beliefs, traditions, and practices. There is no single god, prophet, central set of beliefs, organization, or common document. One of my Hindu co-workers described Hinduism as more of a way of life rather than a religion. This is probably a more appropriate description. Most Hindus believe in some sort of supreme being but don't necessarily worship this being or feel that any one religion is the only way to the supreme being. Various Hindu groups may believe in monotheism (single god), polytheism (multiple gods), or even atheism (no gods). There are however a few common beliefs, including reincarnation, authority of the Indian sacred texts (Vedas) and the priests (Brahmans), and the law of karma. Yoga is a very important practice of Hinduism for both physical and spiritual exercise. Meditating about self to achieve a higher consciousness is another common practice, which is a belief shared along with reincarnation and karma with other Eastern religions and several New Age groups.

Karma is the belief that you get what you deserve, both in this life and the next one. This belief makes Hinduism a religion based on works. Many believe that you can move to a higher class in the next life if you are good in the current life. Likewise, some believe that you could move to a lower class or even be reincarnated as an animal or a plant. At some point, you can exit the cycle of rebirth if you have resolved all of the negative karmas. This allows a believer to reach the maximum level of consciousness where man and god are one.

Buddhism

Buddhism is the one of the world's oldest religions. It is based on the teachings of Gautama Buddha who lived in the fifth century B.C. Like most religions, there are different factions and beliefs in Buddhism that have developed over the years. Buddhism is a non-theistic religion, which means that the religion is built without regard to whether there are any gods. Also, Buddhism is not based on either faith or works, but rather on developing the mind through meditation and self analysis. "Dharma" refers to a path of understanding encompassing the teachings of Buddha to allow one to discover the truth. Followers can obtain peace and happiness by following the teachings of Buddha and using these teachings to obtain a higher consciousness. Most Buddhists believe in karma and reincarnation, but there is no mention of the afterlife. Reaching a state of perfect peace and exiting the rebirth cycle is called Nirvana by many followers. One of the key practices taught by Buddha was called the *middle way*, which means to avoid extreme positions and take the middle ground regarding things that may or not exist. This approach applies to a Buddhist's opinions about God and the afterlife.

Chinese Traditional

Chinese Traditional Religions make up the next largest group, but it is really a misnomer to call these religions. Like Hinduism and Buddhism, there is a wide variety of beliefs, none of which are required. A follower can pick and choose beliefs from different sects. What this group really represents is the cumulative rituals and beliefs that have been practiced by Chinese citizens for thousands of years. The most recognized sets of belief would be classified as Confucianism, Taoism, and Chinese Buddhism. Because the belief sets have existed for thousands of years, there are elements of the following:

- Mythology
- Superstition
- Communication with the earth, moon, sun, and stars
- Communication with animals
- Legends and folklore
- Hundreds of folk gods and goddesses
- Ancestral worship

Many Chinese believe in reincarnation. There are also elements of meditation and self analysis in China brought about by the huge influence of Buddhism. The popular concept *feng shui* used in interior design today is an ancient Chinese practice of using the laws of astrology and the earth to improve one's life through positive energy.

It is difficult to get accurate numbers about religion in China due to the limited access that has been allowed by the Chinese government. However, best estimates are that Hinduism, Buddhism, and Chinese Traditional beliefs added together would result in almost 2 billion followers worldwide. This is a huge number of people looking in a large number of places for their spirituality. Most of the beliefs we have discussed in this section allow the followers to look wherever they feel it is most relevant to them. Each person can choose what he wants to believe, define his god (if any) however he wants to, and satisfy his spirituality needs in any way that seems appropriate. This sounds appealing doesn't it? It describes what is happening with many people in America today!

The New Age Movement

We are covering New Age beliefs separately because New Age is not really a religion but is a loose collection of spiritual beliefs which includes beliefs and practices from many of the religions we just reviewed. New Age is similar to Hinduism in that each believer can pick and choose what he wants to believe. There is nothing more mainstream right now that people picking and choosing what they want to believe!

If you wanted to develop a new religion, how would you go about attracting followers? Why not learn from the politicians? Tell everyone what they want to hear. Let people make up their own rules and define their god however they want to. Get rid of all the talk about sin and ending up in hell. Convince everyone that heaven is a state of mind rather than a place where you can spend eternity. Let everyone know that they can become gods by conquering their minds and getting to a higher level of consciousness. Tell people that the Bible doesn't represent Truth by coming up with contradictory statements. Change Christianity from a religion of submission to God to a religion of empowerment of the individual. Find some admired celebrities to jump on your bandwagon and support your position. You would get a lot of people who would want to check this out! This is exactly what has happened. The new so-called religion is a loose collection of beliefs called New Age. I call it the religion of wishful thinking.

Can you honestly believe in someone who just tells you what you want to hear? I recently heard a talk by a pastor who admitted that he had been fired more than once from church jobs. He attributed his firing to the fact that he just "told it like it is." He didn't sugar coat God's messages in the Bible. He told people what God wanted them to hear, and to some it was offensive. Firing a pastor like this is what we call "shooting the messenger." Do you think that one of the causes for people changing religions so much is to find someone who will tell them what they want to hear? We will look at a survey later in this book that supports this theory.

So exactly what is New Age? It is actually a loose collection of beliefs of numerous groups or individuals. Many of the beliefs have been around for thousands of years because there is a definite similarity to the Eastern religions such as Buddhism and Hinduism. There is no central New Age organization, no clear leader, and no single god. In spite of this, New Age influence increased in the 1970s and took another big step forward in 2008. The term New Age refers to the anticipated time when the world will be governed by a single worldwide government, the entire world will focus on a common agenda and religion, and there will be an end to famine, disease, wars, and poverty. Unification of the world is a major goal of the New Age movement. Having a common religion means that religions such as Christianity and Judaism must be removed or changed to allow for the more Eastern type thinking of the New Age movement.

Let's look at some common New Age beliefs, with the caveat that not all groups believe in all of these theories. Some followers of traditional religions have embraced some of these beliefs in addition to their traditional beliefs. You may not know anyone who considers themselves to be New Age, but you will see later that some of these beliefs are having an impact on our society.

One of the most common New Age beliefs is that god is in everything that exists and everything that exists is god. This redefines God as not really a personal being but some sort of energy or a universal force. This view, commonly called pantheism, means that each of us can become a god by somehow achieving a transformation. Transformation is the personal experience that leads a person to a higher level of consciousness and acceptance of New Age beliefs. The similarity to Buddhism is obvious since both religions allow you to think your way into Nirvana. Many New Age groups also believe in reincarnation and karma, similar to the Eastern religions that developed this concept.

Several New Age groups focus on Mother Earth as a deity. They believe that Mother Earth is a living being that can and should be worshiped since god is in all things and all things are god. The belief that all things are god leads to the concept of universality. Universality is the belief that all religions lead to the same result. Universality could be a major argument by those trying to bring all the world's religions together in the end times. An increasing number of people in the U.S. are supporting the idea that all religions are just different versions of the same basic truths!

Many New Age groups believe that Jesus, Buddha, Muhammad, and other religious teachers were sent here by extraterrestrials. They believe that these extraterrestrials are also gods. New Age channelers say that they are receiving messages from these extraterrestrials. We will discuss the true source of these messages later in this book.

There is also a movement known as the New Thought movement, which is not really part of the New Age movement but shares some similarities. The Unity Church is one faction of this movement that is using Christian concepts and terminology to attract people. According to their website (www.unityonline.org), there are more than 900 Unity churches. The Unity movement believes in an all powerful god, who is *in* everything. The movement supports the divinity of Jesus to the extent that the Spirit of God lived in Jesus the same way it lives in everyone else. Therefore, each person has the same potential to achieve the perfection of Christ like Jesus did. As far as salvation and hell, they teach the following: "Salvation is now--not something that occurs after death. It happens whenever we turn our thoughts from fear, anxiety, worry, and doubt to thoughts of love, harmony, joy, and peace. The 'fall' takes place in consciousness whenever we fall into negative habits of thinking. heaven and hell are states of consciousness, not geographical locations. We make our own heaven or hell here and now by our thoughts, words, and deeds." [1]

So, what types of people are buying into the New Age radical religion where you make your own rules and believe whatever you want to believe? What types of people are looking for something that appeals to their intellectual pride, logical reasoning, and self absorption? What types of people believe that you can move away from Jesus and still get into heaven? What types of people have trouble accepting the simple truths in the Bible? The statistics that we looked at earlier seem to support that many of these people call themselves Christians or were Christians at one time.

The New Age movement promotes appealing intellectual concepts that are difficult to understand and actually harder to believe than some of the miracles in the Bible. Many people are being deceived by this movement which in its simplest form empowers the individual to make God in his own image. God is not an impersonal concept or an intellectual exercise!

Jesus referred to him many times as his Father and our Father. We don't need to take an intellectual approach to believing in God. Furthermore, we don't need to look inside ourselves or at objects that were made by God to find God – we can just look at Jesus.

A big problem with the New Age and all of the various theories that it has spawned is that there is no support for any of these theories. In reality, all of the theories are intellectual positions that various people figured out on their own or borrowed from Eastern religions. The Bible, on the other hand, is based on actual historical events and people who communicated directly with God. These events were well documented by the eyewitnesses who were present when they occurred. As Christians, we believe that everything in the Bible came directly from God to his messengers. The Bible says: "All Scripture is God-breathed and is useful for teaching, rebuking, correcting and training in righteousness, so that the man of God may be thoroughly equipped for every good work." [2]

Current Events

Some of the religious theories we have just looked at have received lots of publicity in the last few years. One platform for presenting spiritual and religious topics has been *The Oprah Winfrey Show*. Oprah Winfrey might be the most influential woman in America and one of the most influential in the world. She is certainly one of the wealthiest and most visible women of our time. You know you are famous when you can be identified by just your first name.

Oprah Winfrey's television show, which recently ended, appeared Monday through Friday on American and international television. Estimates are that her show averaged around 10 million viewers per day just in the U.S., but much larger numbers of people have seen her show at one time or another, read her magazine, or visited her website. Oprah has become a significant spiritual leader in America over the last 10 years, and millions of her fans rely on her for advice. On the main page of her website (as of January, 2013), there was a link for spirit topics. If you clicked on the link for her book club a couple of years ago, you would have seen Eckhart Tolle's book *A New*

Earth: Awakening to Your Life's Purpose, along with information on how to sign up for the online class for this book. This book promotes several New Age and Eastern religion concepts that were mentioned previously in this chapter. According to some estimates, 3.5 million copies of this book were shipped within the first month after Oprah made it a selection of her book club. People have decided that Oprah can help them, and they are more than ready listen to what Oprah says!

I think there is a difference between spirituality and religion. There is nothing wrong with improving your self-awareness, eliminating certain desires from your mind, and learning to deal with your pride and ego. These things are part of your spirituality. It is obvious that the world would be a better place if we all improved our own behavior. Many of Oprah's suggestions and the suggestions of her guests in the spirituality world are certainly helpful. Oprah, who claims to be a Christian, said on one of her shows that Jesus "just can't be" the only way to God. I realize that many of you agree with her statement even though it is contradictory to the Bible. I think God expects us to believe all of his Word. Picking and choosing the parts of the Bible that you want to believe is called making God in your image. When we choose to not believe God, aren't we demonstrating a lack of faith in him?

An example of a book which Oprah has endorsed is Eric Butterworth's *Discover the Power within You.* On Oprah's website, she made this comment about the book – "This book changed my perspective on life and religion. Eric Butterworth teaches that God isn't 'up there'. God exists inside each one of us, and it's up to us to seek the divine within." [3] Pantheism is the concept that God is in each one of us regardless of whether we believe in him or have accepted Jesus as our Savior. This is contrary to the Bible. This book also contains this statement: "The message of the Gospels has been misunderstood. They have been made to appear to say that Jesus was really God taking the form of man…." [4] This statement contradicts the core belief of Christianity.

I think that all Christians should be aware of what is happening here whether you normally watch Oprah's shows or read her magazine or not.

I don't consider Oprah to be a religious expert (and neither am I). I believe that she is intelligent, studies things that she believes can transform her audience, and speaks her mind. She brings people on her shows who are experts in various subjects and allows them to explain their positions. These interviews influence millions of people. We should be wary of getting information about God from any source other than the Bible.

Here are some of the statements that Oprah or her guests have made along with my comments. Most of these statements can seen in videos that are available on www.youtube.com.

- "There are many paths to what you call God. There couldn't possibly be just one way to God." Technically, this is a true statement if you worship a god of your own creation. This illustrates the New Age concepts that God is not a personal being, that God is in each of us, and we can discover our own divinity. So, it is true that if we can invent our own god, then any path would lead to that god. This statement is not true if we worship the God who is our Creator, Lord, and Savior. In John 14:6, Jesus said "I am the way, the truth, and the life. No one comes to the Father except through me." Jesus also said "These words you hear are not my own; they belong to the Father who sent me" (John 14:24).

  There is only one God and he *is* a personal being! He speaks and refers to himself by name: "God said to Moses, 'I am who I am. This is what you are to say to the Israelites: I AM has sent me to you.'" (Exodus 3:14). Jesus refers to God multiple times as his Father, such as in Matthew 18:10: "See that you do not look down on one of these little ones. For I tell you that their angels in heaven always see the face of my Father in heaven." God made us in his image: "So God created man in his own image" (Genesis 1:27). God is not something we define on our own. He is a personal being who desires a relationship with us through his Son Jesus.

- "Jesus came to show us the Christ consciousness." The English word *Christ* comes from the Greek word which means anointed, which in turn came from the Hebrew word for messiah. Jesus is *the* anointed Messiah, sent by God to save us from sin and to reveal the true nature of God. Jesus brings the light that we need to discern the truth. He came to improve our God-awareness rather than our self-awareness. In other words, he came to show us what God is like. Jesus said "Anyone who has seen me has seen the Father. How can you say, 'Show us the Father'?" (John 14:9). Jesus is the Christ, the one and only Son of God. The term Christ is not a job title or a description to be shared by several individuals. We can try to become more like Jesus, but we cannot become Jesus.

• "God is a feeling experience, not a believing experience, because 'God is'." This supports the New Age concept that God is in everything, including each of us, and that we can feel God by obtaining a higher level of consciousness. However, it is impossible for humans to comprehend the majesty of God. Even God, when asked what his name was, said "I Am." This is a way of saying that God's majesty is too great for us to try to give him a human name. God knows our hearts and what we believe. He makes it clear in the Bible that Christianity is a believing experience rather than a feeling experience. "For it is with your heart that you *believe* and are justified, and it is with your mouth that you confess and are saved" (Romans 10:10). "*Believe* in the Lord Jesus, and you will be saved—you and your household" (Acts 16:31). "For God so loved the world that he gave his one and only Son, that whoever *believes* in him shall not perish but have eternal life" (John 3:16).

A New Earth

In the book *A New Earth: Awakening to Your Life's Purpose*, Eckhart Tolle continues the New Age and Eastern religion teachings of trying to find the divinity that is within each of us. I am sure that many of you have read the book and possibly participated in the webcast that further discussed the book. I read this book recently to see why it was so popular. To me, it was like many other self-help books I have read. The book contains some good suggestions for dealing with our egos and some of the unconscious behavior that we all exhibit. There is plenty of need for self analysis in all of us. There are several quotes from the Bible that tend to make the book look like it is consistent with Jesus' teachings. However, the overall message that I discerned in the book is to find the divine that is within us and realize that we are one with God and all other creations. This is a classic New Age teaching that you will miss unless you study each sentence in the book carefully.

Another New Age teaching seen in this book is the one describing heaven as a state of consciousness rather than a location. This statement implies that we can obtain heaven while we are still on Earth. It is true that we can experience many of God's blessings while we are still on Earth, but we cannot obtain heaven as it is described in the Bible until we die. You can probably think your way into some sort of inner peace on earth but not eternal life. The only place you can think your way into is hell.

New Age beliefs don't really support the concept of dying and going to heaven or hell. Instead, they support reincarnation forever. The Bible teaches that heaven is a place where a Christian's spirit goes when he dies and where he will obtain a new heavenly body. God really does live "up there"! Jesus says: "For I have come down from heaven not to do my will but to do the will of him who sent me." [5] You can't come down to Earth from a state of mind! The Bible tells us that Jesus came *down* from heaven to Earth, and ascended *up* into heaven after his resurrection: "While he was blessing them, he left them and was taken up into heaven." [6] The Greek word *ouranos* used for heaven throughout the Bible means in the sky or above the sky.

The Bible also contradicts the theory of reincarnation: "Just as man is destined to die once, and after that to face judgment, so Christ was sacrificed once to take away the sins of many people." [7] The meaning of this passage is clear: we only die once. We don't get a second chance to get it right by coming back to life in a different form.

The New World Order

You may be thinking that we spent a lot of time looking at New Age beliefs when it is technically not even a religion. Yes, we are spending a lot of time on the New Age, and here is why. The New Age movement is helping to prepare the way for the New World Order. What is this? As I said earlier in this chapter, New Age refers to the anticipated time when the world will be governed by a single worldwide government, the entire world will focus on a common agenda and religion, and there will be an end to famine, disease, wars, and poverty. The government that is to reign in the New Age is commonly referred to as the New World Order. Many people speculate that secret meetings are already taking place among world leaders to lay the groundwork for the New World Order. In fact, usage of the term New World Order is becoming common in our society. If you search for this term on the Internet, you will receive millions of results!

The goal of establishing a New World Order is also a goal of the Antichrist in the end times (as influenced by Satan). In fact, the Bible tells us that the Antichrist will be the head of this new worldwide government. The New Age movement is helping to prepare the way for the Antichrist, and we can't stop it because it is part of God's plan for the end times. All we can do is discern the truth and make sure we are on the right side in the spiritual war that is occurring. As Christians, we should be concerned for those who have been or are being deceived, and we should help them determine truth in any way that we can. If you are not sure whether your current beliefs are correct, check them against the Bible.

How to Determine Truth

So, how do we know when we are being deceived, and how do we know if we are hearing the truth? Here are some hints. God made the universe and everything in it. He made the laws of nature, and he made the spiritual laws. He sees the future and knows exactly what is going to happen before it happens. Therefore, the truth is whatever he says it is. God is the absolute authority on truth. But since God is not speaking to us face to face, how do we know whether a particular theory about him is correct or not? This seems to be a big problem for many people in today's society.

Thankfully, God has spoken to us through his Son Jesus and his written Word, the Bible. The answers we need can be found there and they are timeless.

Biblical Warnings

One of the things that we can see in the Bible is God's warnings about the future (including our present time). How did God know that these things would happen? God knows because he is an all-knowing, all-powerful God. He knows the future because he has no limitations. Time as we know it is not the same for God.

Jesus made this statement when speaking about the end times:

> "At that time if anyone says to you, 'Look, here is the Christ!' or, 'There he is!' do not believe it. For false Christs and false prophets will appear and perform great signs and miracles to deceive even the elect—if that were possible. See, I have told you ahead of time." [8]

Jesus is warning us about false Christs and prophets who will appear. There are plenty of false prophets today who want to divert you from the teachings of the Bible. But what about false Christs? There have been several of these already, most notably Jim Jones and Sun Myung Moon. A false Christ is anyone other than Jesus who claims to be Christ.

Jesus also warned us why we need to get our beliefs firmed up before the end times:

> "Be careful, or your hearts will be weighed down with dissipation, drunkenness and the anxieties of life, and that day will close on you unexpectedly like a trap. For it will come upon all those who live on the face of the whole earth. Be always on the watch, and pray that you may be able to escape

all that is about to happen, and that you may be able to stand before the Son of Man [Jesus]." [9]

There are some important points in these verses. First of all, the events in the end times are going to happen, and most people are going to be surprised when they do. The reason is because they will be so focused on their day-to-day lives, material possessions, and pursuit of happiness instead of focusing on God and getting ready for his judgment. Does this describe you? Second, we are going to appear before Jesus and we need to make sure that we are right with him. What does it mean to be right with Jesus? It means that we have accepted him as our Savior and have turned from our lives of sin. It would be embarrassing, and a fatal mistake, to stand before Jesus and have him tell us that he doesn't know us (Matthew 7:21). Jesus tells us about those who won't be taken into his Kingdom when describing the end times in Matthew 13:41: "The Son of Man will send out his angels, and they will weed out of his kingdom everything that causes sin and all who do evil."

Remember this: Jesus says that if we are not *for* him, then we are *against* him (Matthew 12:30). Ignoring Jesus or deferring the decision to accept him as your Savior means that you are rejecting him. God has given Jesus full authority to judge in the end times, and he will judge based on whether we accepted or rejected him (Revelation 20:15).

Do you know people who have put off getting to know and accept Jesus? Are you one of these people? Are you a person who thinks that there are many ways to God other than Jesus?

Guidelines for Determining Truth

How do we decide which beliefs are correct when there are so many opinions being expressed as truth? Why do many people think that organized religion may not have the answers they need? Why do many people think that a politically correct, non-threatening belief system is something they should seek? Is God's Word still relevant for our modern age?

I used to work with someone whose definition of determining truth was to see if something "smelled right." He called this the "smells test." Perhaps you have used this method yourself. It basically consists of applying common sense to a situation to see if it could be true. There are plenty of things that we hear that just don't pass the common sense test. Take the case of Jim Jones. He pulled around 900 people into a cult in the name of religion, but he was allegedly a drug addict, an atheist, and was using the cult to promote communism. His followers killed a U.S. congressman who had come to visit Jones' camp. In 1978, he convinced his followers to drink cyanide, which resulted in everyone committing mass suicide. I am wondering when these people figured out that their situation just didn't smell right.

Unfortunately, the common sense test doesn't work all the time. In the case of God, it just doesn't seem to make sense that he would only provide one way (Jesus) for people to be saved from sin. It just doesn't seem to make sense that God would choose to bless whoever he wants to and not everyone. It just doesn't seem to make sense that God will send everyone who rejects him to hell. However, when we make judgments like this, we are using our definition of common sense rather than God's. God's definition is based on his master plan for humanity.

One way we can determine if someone is truthful is through our history with them. If a person tells us something that turns out to be true, then we tend to believe them more the next time they say something. In God's case, we can see that he is truthful based on the fact that he always fulfills his promises. We can see exactly how God works in the book of Exodus. Moses was pleading with the pharaoh of Egypt to release the Israelites from captivity. The pharaoh was refusing to do so because the Israelites were a valuable workforce. Moses continually warned the pharaoh what God was going to do if the pharaoh did not release the Israelites. God brought significant plagues upon Egypt in hopes that the pharaoh would repent and let the people go. After each plague, the pharaoh hardened his heart and became more stubborn. God did exactly what he promised after each rejection from the pharaoh. The pharaoh refused to acknowledge that the God of the Israelites was more powerful than any of the Egyptian gods. Instead of being impressed by God's power and display of miracles, the

Egyptians cursed him. The final plague brought by God was to kill the firstborn of every family. Israelites were told to spread the blood of a lamb on the door of their houses to indicate their faith in God. Those who did so would be spared, and all who did not do this would have their firstborn killed. God made the choice very clear. They could follow his way, or suffer the consequences. This event, known as the Passover, made it very clear how God gives everyone a choice to accept him or reject him. If we reject him, we suffer the consequences (as the Egyptians did). We can't blame the results on God because they are results of our own actions.

What is truly amazing is that people do not learn from the past. The Bible tells us that scenarios similar to the Egyptian plagues will exist in the end times, but they will be worse. Instead of turning to God, people will harden their hearts and curse him (Revelation 16:9). Instead of accepting God, people will reject him and be condemned forever. God gives us a way out – his Son Jesus, who is also called the Lamb of God. Jesus shed his blood so we could be saved, just like the Israelites who trusted God by using lamb's blood during the Passover event. Do you see why Jesus is called the Lamb of God? His blood saved us from our sins! Did you know that Jesus was crucified on the Jewish Passover holiday, which commemorates the original Passover event in Egypt? Do you think this was just a coincidence or part of God's plan?

So, how do we determine truth? Fortunately, God makes it easy. God's instructions on how to determine truth are set forth in 1 John 4:1-3:

> "Dear friends, do not believe every spirit, but test the spirits to see whether they are from God, because many false prophets have gone out into the world. This is how you can recognize the Spirit of God: Every spirit that acknowledges that Jesus Christ has come in the flesh is from God, but every spirit that does not acknowledge Jesus is not from God. This is the spirit of the antichrist, which you have heard is coming and even now is already in the world."

What does this quote from the Bible really mean? Many people actually acknowledge that Jesus lived on Earth, but don't consider him to be the divine Son of God. Does this mean that the spirits in those people are from God? I don't think so. Satan even acknowledges that Jesus exists, but he certainly doesn't worship him. This passage really means that a spirit that is from God acknowledges that Jesus is the Son of God and is the Messiah that God promised to the Hebrews. Any spirit that tries to twist the truth about Jesus into something else is just not from God. If you believe something that is not consistent with Bible, then your belief is not supported by God.

In the spiritual world, there is good, and there is evil. Anything that is not from God is from Satan. Satan is good at making things sound attractive, but that doesn't change who he is or his evil agenda. We need to recognize that many of Satan's deceptions will be appealing to our sinful natures. This will make them easy to believe, but it will not make them true.

Think about the people who are providing religious guidance to you and see if they meet the test laid out in 1 John 4:1-3. Then, decide whether the Bible is your primary source for information about God. The Bible is truth because it came from God, and God cannot lie.

How important is it to have firm beliefs? If you know people now who are struggling with finding the truth, just wait until the Antichrist shows up in physical form (his spirit [Satan] is already here in the world). There will be intense pressure on everyone to abandon their Christian beliefs and those who are weak or not secure in their beliefs will give in. Of course, the Antichrist may not show up in our lifetimes, but the only chance we have to get our beliefs right is while we are still alive.

We may know who Jesus is, but does he know who we are? Jesus says that whether you get to heaven depends on whether he knows you, not on whether you know him.

> "Not everyone who says to me, 'Lord, Lord,' will enter the kingdom of heaven, but only he who does the will of my Father who is in heaven. Many will say to me on that day, 'Lord, Lord, did we not prophesy in your name and in your name drive out demons and perform many miracles?' Then I

will tell them plainly, 'I never knew you. Away from me, you evildoers!'" [10]

What is the will of the Father in heaven? It is to accept Jesus as our Savior, and to obey him. Jesus tells us this in the book of John: "If anyone loves me, he will obey my teaching. My Father will love him, and we will come to him and make our home with him." [11]

Who Is In Control?

Who is in control of your life? Do you rely on your own intelligence to make decisions or is there a higher power who helps to guide you? Are you buying in to some of the alternate beliefs that we looked at in this chapter? Have you decided that you don't need God because you are doing just fine on your own?

Remember when your parents told you that you had to eat your broccoli (or whatever your least favorite food was)? The conversation probably went back and forth with a few statements and arguments before your parents said: "Because I said so! I make the rules around here!" When we become an adult, we have a completely different perspective than a child. We make rules to protect the child and enable the child to be successful. We do this because we love him. What would happen to a child that ignored all of the rules? Most likely, he would get in trouble, get hurt, have problems in school, have health issues, etc. Would we still love him? Of course we would. Would we allow him to suffer the consequences of his own decisions? Yes, we would because this helps children learn and grow. But we would do everything we could to bring him back to an environment where these issues wouldn't exist.

God is like this. Since God created the universe, our world, and everything that is in it, he has the right to set the rules. He is in charge and he is going to implement his plan that is recorded in the Bible. His plan allows each of us to choose our eternal future. It is up to you to decide whether you are going to participate with God or go your own way. The Bible was given to us for our benefit so that we could be saved from destruction and spend eternity with God. We need to recognize that God's plan is in our best interests, and we aren't going to discover it if we are looking outside the Bible for the answers to life.

God's judgment is based on his definition of the truth – not ours. If you know people that have moved away from him, he is waiting to take them back. All he asks is that we love Jesus, repent, and obey his commandments.

Summary

In this chapter, we have looked at many different beliefs and talked about ways to determine the truth. Here are the key points from this chapter.

- Three major religions, accounting for over half of the world's population, believe in a single God, but don't agree who he is or whether Jesus was his Son.
- Eastern religions and New Age beliefs focus on the spirituality within each individual, rather than a single all-powerful God.
- New Age thinking is receiving significant publicity on television and in print and is influencing millions of people.
- New Age beliefs are drawing people away from traditional Christianity.
- The objectives of the New Age movement are consistent with Satan's objectives.
- The Bible gives us the truth about God.
- The Bible lays out the guidelines for determining whether a spirit is from God.
- Many false prophets have come into the world to deceive us about God.

In the next chapter, we will find out why the Bible is true, who God really is, and why we can believe him.

CHAPTER 4:

The Sources of Truth

As I mentioned earlier, I am writing this book from a Christian perspective. If you are a Christian, we are getting ready to cover a lot of information that you may already be familiar with. Nonetheless, we still need to review this information because it will be referenced later in the book. And, you may learn something as well. The rest of this book is based on the fact that the Bible is God's Word and that Jesus is the Son of God who died for our sins and rose again to join his Father in heaven. In this chapter, we will focus on how we know that these things are true.

We have already seen that many Christians are not that knowledgeable about the Bible and that many of them have beliefs that are directly contrary to the Bible. Some of these beliefs are shared by non-Christians as well. As an example, a 2002 Barna survey discovered the following: [1]

- 59 percent of Americans reject the existence of Satan
- 74 percent say we become sinful based on choices rather than being born sinful
- 42 percent think that Jesus sinned
- 50 percent believe that you can go to heaven by being good (doing good works)
- 44 percent say that the Bible, Qur'an, and Book of Mormon are different expressions of the same spiritual truths

These beliefs are contrary to the Bible! Our beliefs about God need to be based on the truth, and the truth about God is contained in his Holy Word, the Bible. In the Bible, we can see what God says about himself, and also what Jesus says about himself and God. We can also see the historical events that took place that demonstrate the truth about God. Before looking at what the Bible says, let's talk about the Bible and how we know whether the information in it is true.

Can We Trust the Bible?

I have been attending evangelical churches my entire life. Evangelicals believe that the Bible is the inspired Word of God. The more conservative churches feel that every word is correct. It is easy for us to get off track by taking one verse out of context and applying a literal interpretation to it. Instead, the Bible must be interpreted within the context of the time periods in which it was written as well as the remainder of the Scripture to determine its true meaning. So, how do we know if the Bible is true?

First, we need to look at who the authors were. The protestant Bible contains 66 books written by 40 different authors over thousands of years. The most important factor in determining the credibility of these authors is that they were eyewitnesses to the events that occurred, or they had access to those who were eyewitnesses. Usually a historical text is more accurate the closer its creation date is to the time frame when the events occurred. Not only that, but if a book was written at or near the time that the events occurred, there would have been plenty of readers who would have had direct knowledge as to whether the authors' writings were true. It is significant that we haven't discovered any texts that refute the Bible which were written during similar time periods. If any of the biblical books were not considered accurate by those who would have known, surely we would have seen written rebuttals. This is especially true related to accounts about Jesus, because the Jewish leaders wanted to discredit him.

A second factor in establishing credibility of the authors is how amazingly consistent all of the books are. You can read the Bible from front to back and find consistent information throughout as though it were a single book. However, the Bible contains books that were written independently in different time periods. Prophecies in early books show up as being fulfilled in later books. Above all, God's message to us is consistent throughout the entire Bible. In reality, the Bible had one author (God) and 40 different scribes who wrote down his message.

Most Biblical scholars believe the first five books of the Bible were written by Moses (except for the last chapter of Deuteronomy which talks about the death of Moses). What was the source of Moses' information? First and most importantly, he interviewed God! God appeared to Moses on numerous occasions and related to Moses the story of creation, of Adam and Eve and their descendants, of Abraham and his descendants, and so forth. He also gave Moses the Ten Commandments and the early laws that were needed by the Israelites. Second, Moses was an eye witness and participant in all of the events from the time the Israelites left Egypt until they moved into the promised land. Finally, Moses had been a high ranking official in Egypt and would have had access to all of the current documents regarding world history. I am guessing that he was able to ask God some pretty good questions about events that happened before the exodus from Egypt. It doesn't get any more reliable than this.

In the New Testament, the gospels of Matthew, Mark, Luke and John are our primary sources of information about Jesus. These gospels were written independently in the first century. One argument for their authenticity is that they tell many of the same stories in almost identical fashion. Two of the authors, Matthew and John, were disciples of Jesus. They were with him 24/7. They saw and knew things about Jesus that only the disciples experienced. They would surely have known if he was a fake. They wrote what they saw and experienced firsthand. Once again, no writings by anyone who was alive during this time period have been discovered that would refute the message of these gospels. Jesus was witnessed by thousands of people who agreed with the message of the gospels. Even the Jews who rejected Jesus would have trouble arguing that the events described in the gospels did not take place.

Skeptics like to say that various governments or religious officials would have destroyed any contradictory documents. But reality is that none of the first century governments wanted Jesus to succeed. These governments would have destroyed the gospels rather than anything that contradicted them. Christians were widely persecuted during this time, particularly by the Romans. Saying that religious officials would have destroyed competing documents is also problematic in that none of the officials would have had access to them. In the first and second century, books were distributed by hand copying, which resulted in multiple copies being available in different parts of the world. It would have been almost impossible for any group to find all of these copies and have them destroyed. The truth is that competing documents just don't exist.

Christianity is unique among all religions because it is based on historical events rather than philosophical arguments about various theories. The early Christians were anxious to talk about what they had seen and heard, and they did this despite being subject to persecution. Christians today base their beliefs on the fact that these historical events actually took place as described by the eyewitnesses.

Sadly, there are people who are convinced that these events never took place. They have convinced themselves that the events recorded in the Bible were just made up by the early Christians to convince people to believe in their new religion. There is a serious problem with this theory! Why would any human in his right mind invent a religion where the central figure was born to a virgin and was crucified and resurrected from the dead? How could any human invent a scenario like this? It seems that any group of people wanting to start a new religion would come up with something that would be a little easier for people to believe (i.e. fit within their knowledge box). The reason that Christianity spread so fast is that these events were not made up by humans – they actually happened and the people who saw them could not stop talking about what they saw. The Bible is our written record of those events and the eyewitnesses.

Another test of biblical credibility is the prophecy test. The sign of a true prophet is that his prophecies always come true. In the Bible, you will see that all of the prophecies have come true except for those relating to the end times. The reason these prophecies have come true is that they are from God. Any prophecy coming from God is true because he sees the future and can tell us exactly what is going to happen. Many people have a problem with this concept because they say that they have free will to make choices. While that is true, God knows right now what choices we are going to make. You can rest assured that when the end times arrives, the events will be as described in the Bible.

Historical correctness is another way to tell if the Bible is true. You can tell if a book was written as the events occurred by whether references to historical figures, practices, superstitions, and events are correct. Most books will reflect practices and biases that exist at the time they were written. Some of the recently discovered "gospels" such as the gospel of Thomas were actually written in the late second century. It is easy to tell this because they contain references to biblical books that were written in the late first century as well as the influence of practices such as Gnosticism which existed late in the second century. This means that the gospel of Thomas was not written by or about Thomas and could not possibly be accurate. Books written by eyewitnesses tend to stick to the facts. Books written during later time periods sometimes have hidden agendas. All of the books in the Bible pass the historical test.

Another issue we need to address about the Bible is human error. What about errors that may have occurred in the hand copying process over hundreds of years? What about translation errors and misinterpretations of the meaning of Greek or Hebrew words? What about the political agenda of religious groups who worked on translations or decided which books should be included?

Many of these questions can be answered by archeological discoveries. The Dead Sea Scrolls and other discoveries have validated many portions of the Old Testament. As far as the New Testament, there is a complete Greek New Testament manuscript that dates to about 350 A.D, and several significant portions on papyrus that have been traced to the first and second centuries. These manuscripts would allow us to validate any translations or human errors that took place subsequent to that time. As far as the hand copying process, we have reason to believe that it was accurate. The Jews in particular were very meticulous in the copying process. The translation process brings in more judgment since some of the words used in the original language can have multiple meanings. This explains why you will see small differences in some of the biblical translations that we use today. Also, some of the translators seem to have added insignificant phrases or interpretations occasionally. For example, The King James Version refers to Satan as Lucifer. This is the only English translation where the word Lucifer exists, and it is not in the original Greek.

The 2005 book *Misquoting Jesus* makes a case that the Bible contains errors due to the copying and translation process and therefore the Bible can't be trusted. A further review reveals that almost all of these errors are minor and that none of them change the meaning or context of the message. There are only a few cases where someone like King James decided to add something to the original text. Another example that is a mystery is that the last twelve verses of Mark appear to have been added to the original manuscript at a later time. Most Bibles contain a footnote acknowledging that these verses don't appear in the original text, and they certainly don't change the meaning of anything already disclosed in the Bible. Finally, at least one skeptic has noted that the books of Matthew, Mark, Luke and John aren't consistent when they list direct quotes from Jesus. The implication is that these quotes can't be trusted to be accurate. What this really proves is that each of the gospel writers wrote their stories independently based on their own recollection of the events. The basic message of each is the same even though a few words might be different. If all four gospels had the identical language for each quote, then skeptics would be screaming about collusion between the writers. The fact that the quotes are different adds credibility to the fact that these four different authors saw and heard the same thing. We can forgive them if the exact quotes they wrote down thirty or forty years after the actual events occurred have slight differences.

The problem with the theory that the Bible is full of errors is this: none of the so-called errors really matter. Who cares whether Satan's name is Lucifer or not? Does this change who Satan is or what he is trying to do? Do these errors mean that Jesus is not the Son of God? Absolutely not! None of these errors or misinterpretations change the overall meaning and message of the Bible. The Bible is one of the most accurate books ever written. There are no other texts that have had to stand up to the scrutiny given to the Bible for the last two thousand years.

A huge amount of archeological evidence has been accumulated that supports the originality and the message of the Bible. The Bible is easily validated based on original texts, period appropriate authors, and the fact that it is just as true today as when it was written. Furthermore, we have God's word that the Scripture is true. God is the same yesterday, today, and tomorrow. We are the ones who keep changing. Questioning something written by eyewitnesses seems to be another case of people just looking for what they want to believe.

The Proof for Christianity

There are two events in Christianity that are the cornerstone of the Christian faith. These are the virgin birth and the resurrection of Jesus. I know people who claim to be Christian who don't believe in one or both of these events. After all, neither one of them fits into our knowledge boxes. Is it essential to believe in these two events to be Christian? What about all the theories that propose that these events did not happen? Let's examine these individually, because they are important for determining the truth about God.

The Virgin Birth

Many people do not consider belief in the virgin birth to be a requirement for being a Christian. They consider it enough to believe that Jesus rose from the dead and that we can obtain salvation by believing in him. The problem with not believing in the virgin birth is not believing who Jesus really is. If he is the Son of God, then it means he could not have an earthly father. If the virgin birth did not happen, then it means that Joseph was the father, or even worse, someone else. In either case, this would make Jesus an illegitimate child of two human parents. So, we must decide whether Jesus is the Son of God or the son of someone else. If he is the son of someone else, how could he be our Savior? He would be just like any other human who was ever born. And why would God say "This is my Son in whom I am well pleased?" The virgin birth does not fit into our knowledge boxes, but does this mean that it didn't happen?

Here are some arguments that support the virgin birth:

1. <u>Mary was a virgin when she became pregnant</u>. Believe it or not, most young women 2000 years ago actually waited until they got married before having sex. The custom at that time was for women to marry when they were physically able to have children, and many people speculate that Mary could have been as young as fourteen when she became engaged. When Joseph found out about the pregnancy, he seriously considered ending their engagement because he knew he had not slept with her. This is written in Matthew 1:19 by one of Jesus' disciples. This passage confirms that Joseph was not the father. How do we know Mary was a virgin? She said so herself. Luke 1 records the story of the angel Gabriel appearing to Mary to tell her that she was pregnant. Her response was: "How will this be," Mary asked the angel, "since I am a virgin?" [2]

2. <u>God predicted the virgin birth in Isaiah</u>. In Isaiah 7:14, God says through Isaiah: "Therefore the Lord himself will give you a sign: The virgin will be with child and will give birth to a son, and will call him Immanuel." Skeptics like to argue that this sentence referred to an immediate time period rather than the future and therefore we are looking at this verse out of context. But like many passages in the Old Testament, prophecies are not always fulfilled immediately. Skeptics also argue that the Hebrew word used for "virgin" could also mean "a young woman of marriageable age" or just a "young woman." In the Jewish society, all young women of marriageable age were virgins. If they were not, they were stoned. In the context in which this word was used, it clearly means virgin. God predicted this event because he sees the future and it was part of his plan for it to happen. Using the benefit of hindsight, we can see that this is exactly what took place.

3. <u>God's angel told Joseph that the baby would be God's Son</u>. In Matthew 1:20, an angel told Joseph: "Joseph son of David, do not be afraid to take Mary home as your wife, because what is conceived in her is from the Holy Spirit." Once again, a disciple of Jesus wrote this passage. As a disciple, Matthew would have had access to both Jesus and Mary to confirm this story. It was widely accepted as being true at the time, or otherwise we would see first century texts that dispute it. Matthew and Luke independently included the virgin birth story in their first century texts.

Mary confirmed she was a virgin. Joseph confirmed that he had not slept with her. These facts lead us to only one conclusion: God was the Father of Jesus (as God said he was). Why is this so hard to believe? Today, our medical knowledge allows women with fertility problems to have children. Artificial insemination and in vitro fertilization are just two of the techniques that have been used to create thousands of children today, many of whom may be reading this book. Surely God knows much better than we do how to cause a virgin to become pregnant.

The virgin birth is under constant attack by Satan. He wants us to believe that Jesus is not the Son of God so that we will miss out on the salvation that Jesus provides.

The Resurrection

Many books have been written about the resurrection, both for and against. For people who like to look for books that they agree with, they will not have any trouble finding one. All they need to do is decide what their position is and then go find a book on the resurrection that agrees with their position.

I would recommend the book *The Case for the Real Jesus* by Lee Strobel. Lee Strobel is a former legal editor for a major newspaper and a former atheist who decided to research Christianity in detail for the purpose of disproving it. What he found after all of his research is that the evidence for Christianity was overwhelming. He became a Christian and has written several books defending Christianity. In *The Case for the Real Jesus*, he tackles several issues that are current threats to Christianity. He deals with these by examining both sides of the issue without prejudice. He interviews experts in the field, examines historical documents, and applies common sense. In his book, one of the false beliefs that he deals with is that the resurrection never happened.

Here are five reasons that the resurrection is a true event, summarized from his book with a few of my comments added: [3]

1. <u>Jesus was killed by crucifixion</u>. The Roman soldiers carried out these executions. They had done many of them, and they were good at it. In Jesus' case, he was stabbed in the side with a spear which resulted in many fluids draining from his body. He was taken down by a Jew who moved him to a tomb. Even with our current medical technologies, it would be difficult to revive someone who had undergone what Jesus did. There is no way that he would have healed naturally while lying in the tomb. This event was reported by both biblical and non-biblical historians, all of whom confirm that Jesus was executed. There is no doubt that Jesus actually died. The theory that someone other than Jesus was on the cross not only has no evidence to support it, but his mother and some of his closest friends were standing at the foot of the cross watching. They would have known if it wasn't Jesus. The Romans would have known whether it was Jesus also since he was turned over to them by the Roman Governor, Pilate.

2. <u>Jesus appeared to many people after the resurrection</u>. Jesus' disciples believed that he rose and appeared to them. There is both oral and written evidence of this. According to the apostle Paul, Jesus appeared to hundreds of people after his resurrection. Paul would have known many of these people, and they would have been alive at the time of his writings. When the disciples saw Jesus, they saw his wounds and ate a meal with him. This points to a physical resurrection, not some sort of vision that they had. They were so sure that Jesus rose that they were willing to be persecuted and die for their beliefs.

3. <u>Paul was converted to Christianity after seeing Jesus</u>. Paul, formerly known as Saul, was a Jew who had dedicated his life to persecuting Christians, particularly those Jews who believed in Jesus. Saul was firmly convinced that they were following a false messiah. During one of his trips, Saul was blinded by a great light, and Jesus asked him "Why are you persecuting me?" [4] This encounter occurred after Jesus had ascended into heaven. From that point forward, Saul was renamed Paul because of a personal encounter with the risen Jesus. This is significant because Paul had been a foe of Jesus. He would have had no reason to make this story up. Those who believe that the resurrection was a hoax perpetrated by some of Jesus' close followers have no answer for Paul's experience. Paul was so sure of his experience that he also became persecuted for his belief in Jesus.

4. <u>James, the half-brother of Jesus, became a follower after seeing the risen Jesus</u>. Jesus' half-brothers were not followers of his prior to the resurrection. James in particular was known as a pious Jew who followed Jewish law and tradition. There is no mention of any of the half-brothers being at the crucifixion. When Jesus appeared to James after the resurrection, James became a believer and head of the Jerusalem church. This is another case where a non-believer had a complete change of heart after seeing the risen Jesus. There is no doubt that James' encounter was with the risen Jesus. James was his half-brother and surely would have known that he was meeting with Jesus.

5. <u>Jesus' tomb was empty</u>. There is very little debate about this. The empty tomb was witnessed by the women who came to anoint the body of Jesus on the third day. They found the large stone at the tomb's entrance rolled away, the body missing, and the Roman guards gone. These guards could have been executed for allowing anyone to steal the body. The skeptics like to say that Jesus' disciples stole the body. Of course there is no evidence for this. In fact, this argument supports the fact that the tomb was empty. Why would the disciples even consider stealing the

body? No one would believe that Jesus was resurrected unless they actually saw him alive and walking around (which is exactly what happened). Why would the disciples die for something if they knew it was a hoax? Why was the stone rolled back when Jesus could have walked through it if he wanted to? It was rolled back so everyone would see that he was gone.

Do you believe that the disciples stole the body and hid it somewhere so it couldn't be produced as evidence that Jesus was dead? If this happened, then who was the person that looked and talked like Jesus after the resurrection? This person was recognized as Jesus by his closest associates and his own family. In addition, he was able to walk through walls and ascend into heaven in his resurrected body – things that a fake Jesus would not be able to do. This was Jesus himself, not some elaborate scheme to fake a resurrection. If the Romans or the Jews wanted to prevent Christianity, all they had to do was produce a body. They were unable to do so because there wasn't one.

Things That Aren't in the Bible

Have you ever thought about this? There are some things that the Bible just doesn't tell us. Here are just a few:

- What does God really look like, and why doesn't he let anyone see his face?
- Just how big is the universe? Are there other universes?
- Is there life on other planets?
- What do our spiritual bodies look like?
- Can we see our families on Earth while we are in heaven?
- Exactly when will the rapture occur?

I am sure most of you could come up with other questions that you would like to have answered. Have you ever wondered why these questions are not addressed? Why would God keep these things as mysteries? Wouldn't more information help us make a better decision about God? Are you looking somewhere other than the Bible to get information about God?

The answer to these questions is simple. *The Bible doesn't tell you everything about God, but it tells you everything you need to know.* Let's review what these things are. The Bible gives us a clear definition of who God is. We can see that he is our Creator. We can see that sin has been in the world since Satan tempted Eve. God got so upset with the sin that was occurring that he wiped out everyone but Noah and his family with a flood. Then, he made a covenant with Abraham to build a great nation through which he would bless the world and eventually bring a messiah. He delivered the Jews from captivity in Egypt, and he gave them rules to live by only to find that they continually failed him for hundreds of years. Every time he restored the nation of Israel, they would drift away from God and suffer. The behavior of the Jews broke the covenant with God.

To resolve this futility, God sent his Son Jesus, born of a virgin, sinless, to take away our sins for us. Jesus came to provide a new covenant between God and each of us. Jesus was sacrificed on our behalves, rose from the dead, and ascended into heaven. While he was on Earth, he gave us a true picture of what God is like. We can read the eyewitness accounts of much of what Jesus did. We can see how many lives Jesus changed while he was on Earth and how people were willing to die for their belief in him. All we have to do to receive God's grace and eternal life is to accept Jesus as our Savior and Lord. Yet, many of us have failed to do so. Even many who claim to be Christians are straying away from God. The path to hell is wide and many are following it.

Finally, God laid out his plans for the end times, when he will destroy evil once and for all. He will send Jesus back to collect his believers before the final judgment. God will have his way and he will be glorified. He loves us and desires that not a single one of us should perish as stated in 2 Peter 3:9: "The Lord is not slow in keeping his promise, as some understand slowness. He is patient with you, not wanting anyone to perish, but everyone to come to repentance." All of this is covered clearly in the Bible – God's Word. God defines truth, and he cannot lie.

The Bible is true, and it is timeless (still relevant). There is plenty of information in the Bible for anyone to make a decision about God. There simply is no need to look anywhere else. If anyone needs more answers, then he can obtain a personal relationship with Jesus and become filled with the Holy Spirit, who will help him understand God.

Personal Experiences

Some of the things that we learn about God come from personal experiences and our relationships with Jesus. These things not only confirm what God demonstrates in the Bible but also give us additional confirmation that God exists and how relevant he is for our daily lives. When we develop a personal relationship with Jesus, it is amazing how many things happen to us that don't have logical explanations. Sometimes, these things are answers to prayer, and sometimes they are things that we didn't expect.

In the early 1990s, my family and I were residing in Tennessee. The small software business that I had started was not doing too well. The company had lost its biggest customers in the recession of the early 1990s and was not generating enough income for us to live on. I remember that I had exhausted every option that I had to try to generate some income. I had prayed about my situation several times but usually the prayers were asking God for a specific result. One evening, I told God in desperation that I was turning the problem over to him. I just reached the point where everything I tried on my own was not working, so I just decided to let God take care of me his way. The next morning, I got a phone call from a former associate of mine who offered me a job in Florida. I knew that this is what God wanted, and I was pretty desperate at this point. So, we moved to Florida to take advantage of this opportunity. God's answer to my prayer turned out to be much better than all the specific requests that I had wasted my time on.

After we had been in Florida about four years, we made a trip north to see my sister and my parents for Thanksgiving. After Thanksgiving, I drove back to Florida by myself while my wife stayed behind to help out our son who was in college. I remember driving down the Florida Turnpike late on Sunday evening just hoping that I would make it back without falling asleep. I was playing some music and not thinking about anything in particular other than how nice it was to see my family and how much I missed them.

Suddenly, a voice told me that it was time to quit my job. I remember thinking: "Where did that come from?" It was so convincing, I didn't have to even think about it. I knew that the message was from God, but I am not sure why. I had been thinking that we needed to stay another year, which would give me time to plan how to make sure I had income lined up before leaving my current job. But, God's message was so strong! He said that I needed to leave right now! Based on my previous experience with him, I knew that I needed to listen. After all, I was there because God had answered my prayer previously. First thing the next morning, I went to see my boss and told him I was leaving. I gave him about a three month notice so both of us could make plans. Later in the day, I called my wife and told her that I had quit my job. (Note to husbands: normally, you should discuss this before you quit!) I am sure my wife thought I had gone crazy. She had just seen me the day before, and there was no discussion of this at all. On top of that, I didn't have a new job lined up, and there were no prospects that I knew of for the small business I owned. This is one of the most unusual, yet most faithful, decisions that I have ever made. I had a difficult time explaining it to my family.

Of course, God's plans are not always the same as our plans. His plans are always better! Within a couple of months, my small business got a large new contract for work, and I was hiring contractors to help the business meet its commitments. The day after my three month notice expired, a customer introduced me to the President of a company that was selling to the same industry that I was. At the time I quit my job, I had never heard of this company. We determined that our software products and services were complementary, so we started to do joint marketing and software development. Both of our businesses expanded rapidly. God took my company from one employee to forty in about a year and a half. We ended up merging the two software companies and then selling them to a large conglomerate. Instead of my being bankrupt today, God blessed me financially because I followed his plan for me. I allowed God to take control of my life, and he has taken me places where I never would have gone on my own.

When these events occurred in the early 1990s, I was teaching a Bible Study class and was a deacon in my church. Now that I look back on what happened, I realize that I was a Casual Christian. I had accepted Jesus, but most of my decisions on a day to day basis were made on my own. I relied on him only when I was desperate. I did not realize that God wanted to be involved in my entire life. God was trying to build a relationship with me, and I wasn't paying attention. I feel that many of you are just like I was. I am so glad that God woke me up because I didn't realize that I was missing out on his blessings. If you are in a similar situation, please don't wait as long as I did to come to your senses. God wants relationships!

When God put the idea in my head to write this book, I just knew that I needed to do it!

The point of all this is that learning about God is not just an exercise in reading or studying. We need to experience God as well. These experiences come naturally as a part of our relationships with him. These experiences confirm for us that God is exactly who he says he is and that his Word is true. These experiences show us that God is alive and active in our daily lives and that his plans for us are better than our own.

I became a Christian at about age ten, but I was forty-five before I gave up trying to ask God for things I wanted instead of things he wanted. As I just explained, the results were dramatic. If you are not communicating (i.e. praying) with God on a regular basis, you are missing out on one of God's greatest blessings.

Summary

Here are the major things that we learned in this chapter:

- The Bible tells us everything we need to know about God.
- The Bible is true because it consists of eyewitness accounts that were written while they could still be validated.
- The prophecies in the Bible have come true except for those which will come true during the end times.
- God can appear in physical form if he chooses.
- Recent "gospels" that have been discovered do not belong in the Bible.
- God is our Creator, the all powerful Lord of the universe.
- Nothing is impossible for God.
- We refer to some of God's works as miracles because they don't fit into our knowledge boxes.
- We can learn more about God by having a personal relationship with him.
- God's plans are better than our plans.

CHAPTER 5:

What Do We Know About God?

Beginning with this chapter, we are going to be learning more about the spirit world. The spirit world consists of God, Jesus, the Holy Spirit, and the angels which were created by God. Some of these angels, including Satan, rebelled against God and are now evil spirits and demons who are on Earth. Studying this information should help you decide why you believe what you believe and whether your beliefs are correct.

Let's start with God. Have you ever stopped to think how magnificent God really is? God's Word tells us that he created the heavens and the earth. This doesn't mean just our sun, moon, and the planets in our solar system – it means all of the heavens. Do you know how big our universe is? It is almost impossible to describe in human terms because it has no known boundaries, but let me give you just a few numbers. We live in a galaxy called The Milky Way. Scientists have estimated that our galaxy contains about 100 billion stars and that the universe contains between 100 billion and 500 billion galaxies! The Milky Way is just a speck of dust compared to the overall size of the universe. Yet, traveling at the speed of light, it would take 100 thousand years to go from one side of the Milky Way to the other.

Those are impressive numbers, but not as impressive as this: God is concerned about each of us as individuals! The Bible says that even the hairs on our heads are numbered. God is our Creator – big enough to rule the universe and personal enough to love us as individuals. Our attempts to make God into what we want him to be are certainly futile. As we review the facts about God, think about how they relate to your current beliefs.

Who is God?

Are you one of the people who think that God is just some sort of energy force or nebulous spirit who is everywhere and in everything rather than believing that he is an actual being? Do you believe that God is just whatever you want to believe? If we really want to know who God is, we can just look at the Bible. For all the reasons listed in the previous chapter, the Bible contains truth. God makes it very clear who he is in the Bible. We can learn who he is by reading his own statements as well as studying his behavior. There is just no reason to try to look anywhere else for information about God. In spite of this, people continue to adopt beliefs about God that have no factual basis and directly contradict some of God's statements in the Bible. These false beliefs might make people feel good, but feeling good won't get them into heaven.

Here are things we can learn about God from the Bible:

- *God is the supreme being in the universe.* One of the Ten Commandments is that we should have no other gods before God. [1] God makes it clear that he is the highest power in the universe and he intends to be worshiped accordingly. God makes it clear that *nothing* in our lives should be more important than he is. In our modern society, some of our gods are money, possessions, careers, and selfishness. Most of our gods come from a focus on self.

- *God has feelings like we do.* God was extremely upset during the time of Noah because of how corrupt man had become. He was angry, regretful, and not proud of his creation – so much so that he wanted to wipe out all of humanity. [2] Noah was faithful to God and was spared by God because of his faithfulness. Those who were not faithful were destroyed in the flood. This should teach us that God rewards our faithfulness and punishes our unfaithfulness.

- *God is eternal and has no limitations.* When Moses asked God what his name was, God replied "I Am Who I Am". [3] The Hebrew word for God's name was *Yahweh* which translates to "I will be what I will be." Today, many of our Bible translations use the word "Lord" instead of Yahweh. Do you think that God thought Moses was asking a strange question? God is too big to have a name, and he does not need to be, and will not be, reduced to our level. God was also using this opportunity to tell Moses that he was an eternal God. Yahweh is a first person, present, and future tense word. God is referring to himself as a single being who exists now and forever. When we create our own definitions of who God is, we are reducing his power, holiness, and majesty.

- *God is Holy and is going to demonstrate his Holiness to everyone.* God told the Israelites that he would demonstrate to the entire world that he was Holy by revealing himself through the nation of Israel. [4] To say that God is Holy means that he is separated from sin. God defines everything that is perfect and good. On the other hand, sin was created by angels who rebelled against God. God's promise to Israel was fulfilled when Jesus came into the world, and it will also be fulfilled during the end times.

- *God is the Father of Jesus.* One confirmation of this occurred when Jesus was with Peter, James, and John and was speaking with Moses and Elijah. God spoke in a voice from a cloud, saying "This is my Son, whom I love." [5] God also demonstrated during this event that there are no limitations in the spirit world and that he is in control. A similar confirmation from God came when Jesus was baptized.

- *God is our Creator who created us in his image.* In the early part of Genesis, God tells us that he created man in his own image. [6] God is a spirit rather than a physical being, so how could he create us in his image? The answer is that he created us with a spiritual nature. He created us to be like him in certain respects, but we can never be equal to him because he is our Creator and he is sinless. We can see in the Bible that many of the emotions we have, such as happiness, anger, mercy, rejoicing, patience, and love, are also displayed by God.

- *God is Creator of the universe and everything in it.* God tells us that he created the heavens and the earth and all the living things. [7] Thinking that this happened accidentally or through evolution is harder to believe than just accepting that God did it. The more we learn about DNA and the mysteries of life, the more we should appreciate God's incredible design. This design reveals a power and intelligence way beyond our understanding. God's attention to details was perfect.

- *God is a spirit.* Jesus tells us in the book of John that God is a spirit, and we must worship him in spirit and truth. [8] God is not physical like we are but is a spirit who can be present everywhere at the same time. The magnificence and scope of God is beyond human description or understanding. When God appears to us in physical form, it is usually through his Son Jesus. He sends his Holy Spirit to live in us when we accept Jesus as our Savior.

- *God reveals himself to us through his Son Jesus.* The Bible says that we can't truly know the Father (God) unless Jesus reveals him to us. [9] Bringing ourselves to a higher level of consciousness is still not going to get us to the level of Jesus. We can understand the Father best by looking at the Son, and information about the Son is readily available in the Bible.

- *God loves us and desires that none of us should perish.* Jesus tells a parable in the Bible that illustrates how God rejoices when a person is saved from eternal damnation. [10] God does not wish for *any* of us to perish. However, this does not mean that all ways lead to God, and it does not mean that all people will be saved. God's plan for our salvation is clearly defined in the Bible as accepting his Son Jesus. Those who chose not to do this will spend eternity separated from God.

- *Nothing is impossible for God.* We know this because Jesus tells us this. [11] Things that seem to be impossible to us are not hard for God. This may be hard to believe but it is true. How could there be any limitations for the God who created the universe? Why do many people continue to attach limitations to God by selectively believing what he says?

Is there something in your past or your knowledge box that keeps you from believing these things?

Proof for God

For those who might be skeptical about God, let's take a common sense approach to some stories in the Bible that prove God's existence -

- First of all, God appeared to Moses in person. He would not let Moses see his face because the light was blinding. He spent forty days and nights with Moses giving him the Law and revealing who he was. He spoke with Moses, and many times in the Old Testament, it tells of the loud sounds that were made when God appeared (Exodus 19:18). It was so impressive that the people were afraid of God and told Moses they would do whatever God said. The people did not see God directly, but they saw his power and majesty.

- Second, God (in the form of Jesus) and two angels also appeared to Abraham in human form and Abraham fed them and talked with them (Genesis 18). This event occurred when God was getting ready to destroy Sodom and Gomorrah. Scriptures that you can investigate to learn about Jesus' physical appearances in the Old Testament include Genesis 17:1, 26:24, 35:9; Exodus 3:16; and 2 Chronicles 1:7. Scriptures that document God's speaking to Moses can be found in Exodus chapters 9 through 13. Of course, the ultimate example of God appearing and speaking is through Jesus' life on earth as recorded in the New Testament. These recorded events all support the fact that God is an actual being and not just some sort of energy force or concept.

In addition to physical appearances and sounds, God performed many miracles. We call these things miracles because they are beyond our capabilities and understanding of natural laws (which makes them supernatural). These miracles include the creation of the universe (Genesis 1 and 2), the burning bush (Exodus 3), the ten plagues of Egypt (Exodus 7 through 12), death of the firstborn in Egypt (Exodus 12), the cloud and pillar of fire that led the Israelites in the desert (Exodus 13 and 14), parting of the Red Sea and drowning the Egyptian army (Exodus 14), getting water from a rock (Numbers 20), the sun and moon staying still (Joshua 10), Elijah ascending into heaven (2 Kings 2), and many more. Then there are all the miracles that God performed through Jesus that are documented in the Gospels of Matthew, Mark, Luke, and John. These include healing the sick, driving out demons, raising the dead, Jesus walking on water, Jesus disappearing through an angry crowd, feeding thousands of people with a few pieces of food, turning water into wine, and more. All of these miracles were witnessed by many people and were documented in writing by eyewitnesses. Then of course there are the miracles of the virgin birth and the resurrection, which were explained previously.

Isn't it easier to believe that God caused all these things to happen than to believe that they were just some sort of random events or that people just fabricated these stories? Don't these events prove that God is real? If you choose to not believe in some of these miracles, aren't you defining your own God versus the one described in the Bible?

How Does God Think?

We can look at the Bible plus study our own human nature to figure out how God thinks. God is our Father, and he probably feels similar to how any father would feel for his children. God has rules that he expects us to follow. He wants nothing but the best for us. He expects us to love him, obey him, believe in what he says, and spend time with him. When we move away from God, we are disciplined. If we ask for forgiveness, we are forgiven. If we ask for salvation, we receive it. What a wonderful God! If you have children, think about how much you love them. Think about how you feel when they obey or disobey. Think about how it hurts you to discipline them. Think about how good it feels when they ask for forgiveness. Then, think about how God views you right now based on your relationship with him.

Why would God provide salvation as a free gift? Why wouldn't God just give us a bunch of rules to follow and then grade us on how we did? These are interesting questions that many people have trouble dealing with. Here are some reasons why God did not provide a rule-based system:

- We could actually obey a set of rules without believing in God. For example, you could go to church 75 percent of the time, pray before each meal, avoid the major sins, and claim a high score on the rules compliance test. But you could do all of this without actually believing in God or loving him.

- A rules based system would become legalistic. We would have the same problem the Jews had in following the laws given by Moses. Human interpretation created Jewish legalists whose job was to interpret the laws and decide what a person was allowed to do. There were so many rules that it was impossible to follow them.

- We have a sin nature. We are born with a sin nature and the only way we can get forgiveness for it is from God. This forgiveness is available for free if we just ask for it. The result is eternal life in heaven. We can't earn our way out of being sinful by following rules or doing good works.

Are you being deceived by some of the modern theories that Satan and heaven are not real? Are you being deceived by the theory that you can go to heaven just by being a good person? Are you a believer in the popular theory that we are born as good people rather than sinners? These theories are contrary to the Bible, and therefore they are not true.

Where is God?

In December, 2012, a gunman entered an elementary school in Connecticut and killed twenty innocent children and six adults. When things like this happen, people start asking "where is God". Many want to know why God wouldn't prevent something like this. In other words, they are trying to assign blame for this event to God! First of all, we need to recognize that God gave us free will to make decisions on our own. He is also allowing Satan to roam on Earth until he meets his ultimate destruction in the end times.

We live in a society where two-thirds of the population claims to believe in God but don't allow him into their daily lives. They rely on their own wisdom and strength until they encounter something that is too big for them to handle. Then they want to call on God and have him come to the rescue. We have spent the last fifty years removing God from our schools, our governments, our morals, and our day to day lives. We have pushed him aside and put him on the shelf until we need him. Doesn't it seem silly to ask the question "where is God"? Do you think God approves of being pushed out of our society and being called back only when we are desperate? Instead of dealing with serious spiritual problem that we have in this country, people are talking about gun control, mental illness issues, dangerous drugs, and violent entertainment that cause people to become evil. In other words, we are talking about treating the symptoms rather than the disease. Satan is the one who causes evil, and we cannot defeat him on our own. Only God is more powerful than Satan!

The real answer to the "where is God" question is this: God is wherever you have put him. Either he is involved in your life, or he isn't. He wants to have a relationship with you all the time, not just when it is convenient for you. The Bible tells us in many places that God is always waiting on us to take him back into our lives.

Who is Jesus?

Let's explore what the Bible says about Jesus. The Bible says that Jesus is the Son of God, sent to Earth to become fully human and sacrifice himself for forgiveness of our sins. Jesus was crucified, died, and rose from the dead on the third day. There is very little argument that Jesus actually existed, but only Christians believe that he was the Son of God.

Jesus was both fully human and fully God. This is a confusing concept, but Jesus was born to a human mother and experienced human life just like the rest of us. He learned how we all feel and how we are tempted. He prayed to God and had faith in God. He used God's strength to resist sin. He was able to bear our sins on the cross because of his obedience to God's will! Most of all, he did these things because he loves us unconditionally.

The Bible defines for us who Jesus is:

- *Jesus is God's Son and messenger to the world.* Jesus tells us that he is not doing anything on his own account but rather is delivering messages to us from God, his Father. [12] Jesus says that we will know that he is the Son of God when he is "lifted up" (when he is resurrected). He defines God as his Father many places in the Bible.

- *Belief in Jesus results in eternal life.* In probably the most famous verse in the New Testament, Jesus makes it clear that he is God's only Son and that anyone who believes in him will have eternal life. [13] This is the essence of Christianity. Jesus did not come to condemn us but to save us. Yet there are many people who are threatened by this statement because they think that Jesus only came to criticize everyone, and they reject Christianity because they think Christians are too judgmental. People are turned off by the "holier than thou" attitude that some Christians have. The truth is that Jesus brings a positive message about how we can be saved along with God's expectations for us. He does not criticize those who haven't accepted him yet - instead, he invites them to trust in him.

- *Jesus is the Messiah that was promised to the Israelites.* Jesus tells the Jews that he did not come to abolish the law (Torah) but to fulfill it as the promised Messiah. [14] This is a direct message to the Jews who were so focused on the specifics of the law that they missed the fact that Jesus was fulfilling prophecy. Jesus is making it clear that he is the Messiah that the Jews have been waiting on.

- *Jesus came to save everyone, not just the Jews.* Jesus says that he "has other sheep that are not part of this sheep pen." [15] This is a message from Jesus to the Gentiles (non-Jews). He is stating that he came to save the entire world and not just the Jews. God demonstrated his Holiness by blessing the entire world through the nation of Israel. The important point for us is that Jesus came for our benefit regardless of our nationality, race, or current religious beliefs.

- *Jesus is God incarnate.* Jesus said "I and the Father are one." [16] We use the word *incarnate* to mean that God came to Earth in human form. This also means that Jesus is one form of God. This is not the same as the New Age belief that God is in everything. God created everything but is not in everything. When we accept Jesus, we receive the Holy Spirit who then lives in us. This is the only way we can say that God lives in us.

- *Jesus is the only way to God.* Jesus says specifically that "no one comes to the Father except through me." [17] We have already seen that we can't fully understand God unless we understand Jesus. This solves our problems with not understanding the spirit world very well. Jesus can say that he is the only way to God because he was sent by God to save us from our sins. John 1:1 says that Jesus existed with God in the beginning, and that he *is* God. John 5:23 says that anyone who does not honor Jesus does not honor the Father who sent him. God has not given us any other saviors, laws, or methods by which we can obtain eternal life.

- *If you reject Jesus, you will be rejected in heaven.* Jesus tells us that he will acknowledge us before God if we have acknowledged him, but he will disown us if we have not acknowledged him. [18] This is a pretty clear statement. If you reject Jesus when you are on Earth, then you will be rejected from heaven. If you accept Jesus while you are alive, then you receive access to heaven. If you do not accept Jesus, then you have rejected him. Heaven is not a state of mind but rather a place where a Christian's spiritual body will reside after the physical body is dead.

- *Jesus is eternal.* Jesus tells us that he existed before Abraham was born. [19] Jesus is in the past, present, and future just like God. He used the term *I Am* as a direct reference to the fact that God called himself I Am to Moses. Jesus can say this because he is from God, and is God. Jesus is the physical representation of God. The Bible says that "Jesus Christ is the same yesterday and today and forever." [20] This is a reminder that Jesus has been around since before the creation of the world and will be here after it is destroyed in the end times. Jesus does not change, so when we don't feel as close to him as we should, it is because we changed!

- *Jesus was sinless.* Jesus came to us as a sinless person who was our substitute for paying the penalty of sin. [21] Jesus did not have a sin nature and did not sin while he was on the earth. He relied on the strength of God to resist temptation. In spite of his sinless nature, he agreed to die on the cross to carry all of our sins on our behalves. If we don't allow Jesus to pay the penalty of sin for us, then we will have to pay this penalty ourselves. The penalty for sin is eternal separation from God in hell.

- *Jesus can protect us from Satan.* A major reason that Jesus came was to destroy the devil's work. [22] Jesus' death and resurrection gives each of us the opportunity to be forgiven of our sins and secure eternal life in heaven. Only Jesus can protect us from Satan and eternal misery in hell. We are doomed to defeat if we try to fight Satan on our own.

- *Jesus was crucified and rose from the dead.* When the women went to the tomb to anoint the body, they were alarmed to find the stone rolled away and the tomb empty. [23] The resurrection demonstrates the power of God. We know that the body had not been stolen because Jesus subsequently appeared to many people.

- *Jesus is in heaven.* After the resurrection and after appearing to many people, Jesus ascended into heaven. [24] The disciples were witnesses to this event. The significance of this is that Jesus is still alive and is in heaven waiting on us. He is not just a historical figure who lived two thousand years ago. He is God incarnate, and he lives forever.

- *Jesus is coming again.* Jesus tells us specifically he is preparing a place for us and will come again to take us to heaven.[25]

There are many more verses that I could refer to, but the message is still the same. Jesus is the Messiah that was promised in the Old Testament. He fulfilled hundreds of prophecies exactly as they were written. Jesus came to reveal God and save us from hell. He died on the cross, and rose on the third day. He appeared to many people after the resurrection, and then ascended into heaven. This is documented in authentic historical documents by eyewitnesses, and it is true. There are no valid facts which are supported by evidence that would lead us to believe that Jesus is not the Son of God.

Is Jesus the Only Way?

Do you believe Jesus' statement "I am the way and the truth and the life. No one comes to the Father except through me"? [26] The Spirit of God lived in Jesus, so this statement is coming directly from God. To people who are not Christians, it is probably the most offensive statement in the Bible because it clearly says that other religions do not lead to God. As we have seen, a recent survey found that the vast majority of Protestants feel that *many* religions can lead to eternal life. Many of you might be part of this majority. Perhaps you think that it is just not logical or fair for Jesus to be the only way to God. Perhaps you think that God loves everyone and he would not be that restrictive. Perhaps you believe that Jesus was just a messiah for the Jews and his statement only applies to them. Perhaps you believe that Jesus' statement only applied to the people who were living while he was on Earth. When we talked about thinking outside of the box, what did you discover about yourself that affects what you believe? Are there other things in the Bible that you don't believe? If you knew for sure that Jesus was the only way to God, how would it affect you? I think we need to deal with Jesus' statement, especially for those of you who call yourselves Christians.

My pastor says that if we don't believe Jesus, we are calling him a liar. This is a little harsh, but it is true. Either Jesus was telling the truth or not. Look at it this way: If Jesus really is the only way to God, then what would Satan like for us to believe about Jesus? Satan's agenda is to pull everyone away from God. There is no truth in Satan – when he lies he is speaking his native language (John 8:44). He puts lies in front of us and makes them attractive. He wants us to think that Jesus is *not* the only way to God so we will look somewhere else for God. Based on the statistics that show that people are moving away from Christianity, it looks like Satan is doing a good job. Satan tells lies that directly contradict statements in the Bible or spins them into something with a different meaning. Here is the danger: If we pick and choose the portions of the Bible that we want to believe, we will likely start looking somewhere else to support our positions on the portions of the Bible that we don't believe in. This in turn will divert our attention away from God and result in beliefs that are not based upon the truth.

I realize that many of you who are Christians are secure in your salvation. That is, you have accepted Jesus as your Savior and know that you have been saved. Yet, some of you may still believe that there are other ways to God. The problem with this belief is that you are ignoring the needs of relatives, friend, neighbors and co-workers. Perhaps you think that what these people believe is none of your business. It bothers me to know that I have information that could save someone's life but I am not sharing it with them. This is one of the major reasons that I am writing this book. As Christians, we should reach out to these people and follow Jesus' commandment in Matthew 5:16. Jesus tells us that Christians are the light of the world and that we should let our lights shine so that others will see and glorify God.

The Bible tells us that we are all sinners because we were born that way. Our sins separate us from God, and we cannot be reconciled to him unless our sins are forgiven. Jesus took all of our sins on his shoulders when he died on the cross, and he has paid the price for each of us. No one else has done this, which means that he is the only way that we can be forgiven. When we accept Jesus as our Savior, it means that the separation between us and God is removed. God has not provided us with any other method of reconciling to him.

I know that some of you still think that God would not send anyone to hell, and that he would provide many ways for us to get to heaven. In other words, you have decided that God is going to take the politically correct approach that doesn't offend or exclude anyone. Sorry, but that is just not how God works. Some of our governments have done a good job of leading people into thinking that political correctness is the basis for rules, but there is a big difference between God and our governments. God alone has the authority to decide who will be admitted to heaven and how they will get there. God has told us clearly in the Bible that Jesus is the only way to heaven. You may not think this is politically correct, but it is God's plan for our salvation.

For those of you who think you will go to heaven because you are a good person, your beliefs are directly contrary to what God says in the Bible. In fact, God says that there is no such thing as a good person in Romans 3:23-24: "For *all* have sinned and fall short of the glory of God, and are justified freely by his grace through the redemption that came by Christ Jesus." Regardless of how good you think you are, or how you compare yourself to others, God defines you to be a sinner. This fact automatically separates you from God until you allow Jesus into your heart.

Who is the Holy Spirit?

Since God is Holy, and God is a Spirit, then who is the Holy Spirit, and why is the Holy Spirit referred to as a separate being? The first and most obvious reason is that this is how God wants it, but we still need to understand why. Look at it this way: Jesus came to Earth in human form to show us what God is like. The Holy Spirit comes to Earth in Spirit form to show us what God is like and to help us communicate with him and understand him. The Holy Spirit inhabits Christians' spirit nature to serve as a bridge between us and God.

When people pray to God, they are praying in their natural language. Have you ever wondered how God could understand all of our languages at the same time? Well, this is certainly something he could do. But communication with God involves our hearts and our thoughts as well as our language. God knows what we are thinking as well as what we are saying. Jesus tells us this in Luke 16:15: "He said to them, 'You are the ones who justify yourselves in the eyes of men, but God knows your hearts.'" The Holy Spirit takes our thoughts and feelings and relays them to God. In some cases, the Holy Spirit can express things on our behalf that we are unable to express ourselves (Romans 8:26-27). What we think and feel is more important than the language we are using.

The Bible tells us these things about the role and existence of the Holy Spirit:

- *The Holy Spirit communicates with us on behalf of God.* One example is that a man named Simeon was told by God through the Holy

Spirit that he would not die before seeing the Messiah. [27] When Simeon saw the child Jesus, he praised God because it had been revealed to him that Jesus was the Messiah.

- *The Holy Spirit is a gift from God.* The Bible tells us that God will give us good and perfect gifts when they are within his will. [28] The Holy Spirit is a free, perfect gift from God that we receive when we receive Jesus Christ as our Savior and Lord.

- *The Holy Spirit lives with us.* Jesus tells us that the Holy Spirit would be sent by God after Jesus ascended to heaven. [29] The Holy Spirit therefore becomes the form of God that lives among us. The Holy Spirit reveals things to us about God and the spirit world that are just too hard to understand on our own. We receive wisdom and understanding about God this way.

- *The Holy Spirit intercedes for us.* The Bible says that the Holy Spirit intercedes for us with God by knowing our hearts and thoughts. [30] Sometimes we aren't smart enough to know what to pray for, or we don't pray when we should. Isn't it great that the Holy Spirit intervenes on our behalves? The Holy Spirit is like a guardian angel living in our bodies.

- *The Holy Spirit empowers us.* Jesus told his followers that they would receive powers when the Holy Spirit lived in them. [31] In the early church, believers were anointed with the Holy Spirit and were able to perform miracles, drive out demons, and preach the message about Jesus confidently. In the event known as Pentecost, the Holy Spirit descended on the disciples and their associates like tongues of fire. [32] They were immediately able to speak in languages other than their own. These languages were clearly understood by the crowds they spoke with after this event. The Holy Spirit enables us to do things that we just can't do on our own.

- *The Holy Spirit comes only from belief in Jesus.* The apostle Peter said "Repent and be baptized, every one of you, in the name of Jesus Christ for the forgiveness of your sins. And you will receive the gift of the Holy Spirit." [33] The Holy Spirit comes *only* to those who believe in Jesus Christ and confess that he is Lord.

If we look at all the scriptures supporting God, Jesus, and the Holy Spirit, it is hard to conclude that God is just some sort of energy force that permeates the universe and is part of us. God is exactly who he says in all the forms that he has chosen to reveal to us. The evidence for God is overwhelming. There is no evidence that proves that he doesn't exist or that the information about him in the Bible is not true. There is no evidence that proves that Jesus is not the Son of God, born of a virgin, who died and rose from the dead on the third day. There is no evidence that anyone can obtain eternal life in heaven through any other means other than trusting in Jesus. There is also no evidence that anything God tells us in the Bible is no longer applicable for us. God is timeless, and so is his plan for us.

Summary

Here are the major things that we learned in this chapter:

- God is the Creator of the universe and everything in it.
- God made us in his image.
- God sent his sinless Son Jesus to show us what God is like.
- We can obtain eternal life with God only by believing in Jesus.
- If we reject Jesus or fail to accept him, he will reject us in front of God.
- Jesus was sinless, was crucified, and rose on the third day.
- Jesus appeared to many people after his resurrection and ascended into heaven.
- Jesus is the head of God's church, and all authority has been given to him.
- Accepting Jesus is the only way that God has given us to be forgiven of our sins and obtain eternal life.
- Jesus came to save *all* people who will accept him.
- The Holy Spirit communicates for us with God and helps us understand God.

CHAPTER 6:

What Are Angels?

In a previous chapter, we talked about how we don't fully understand the spirit world. We can improve our understanding by studying some of the members of the spirit world. A better understanding of the spirit world will help you evaluate your beliefs about God. In this chapter, we will focus on angels. What are angels? What are their capabilities? What do they look like? Are they physical, spiritual, or both? Where are they? Do they still exist? If so, what is their role in God's kingdom? Do we have guardian angels?

Billy Graham relates the following story in his classic book *Angels*:

> The Reverend John G. Paton, pioneer missionary in the New Hebrides Islands, told a thrilling story involving the protective care of angels. Hostile natives surrounded his mission headquarters one night, intent on burning the Patons out and killing them. John Paton and his wife prayed all during that terror-filled night that God would deliver them. When the daylight came they were amazed to see that, unaccountably, the attackers had left. They thanked God for delivering them. A year later, the chief of the tribe was converted to Jesus Christ, and Mr. Paton, remembering what had happened, asked the chief what had kept him and his men from burning down the house and killing them. The chief replied in surprise, "Who were all those men you had with you there?" The missionary answered, "There were no men there; just my wife and I." The chief argued that they had seen many men standing guard

– hundreds of big men in shining garments with drawn swords in their hands. They seemed to circle the mission station so that the natives were afraid to attack. Only then did Mr. Paton realize that God had sent his angels to protect them. The chief agreed that there was no other explanation.[1]

Perhaps you don't believe this story, but there are many stories just like this one. Many of these stories report beings who appear, do a good deed, and then disappear. As we will see in this chapter, this type of behavior is typical of angels.

The Characteristics of Angels

The interest in angels seems to have picked up during the last few years as reflected in a number of books that have been written.

I call angels the worker bees of heaven. They were created to do God's work. Most biblical scholars believe that angels were created before God created the earth. This makes sense since the angels could have been used to help God with many tasks that needed to be done after the world was created.

We know that angels existed during the time of Adam from this verse in the Bible: "When men began to increase in number on the earth and daughters were born to them, the sons of God saw that the daughters of men were beautiful, and they married any of them they chose." [2] This verse will be discussed in more detail later in the book, but for now we need to talk about what the term *sons of God* means. Theologians like to argue this point, but the vast consensus is that sons of God means angels. The term used in this verse is consistent with the term used to denote angels in other parts of the Bible. Adam was technically a son of God because he had no earthly father. But all of Adam's descendents had earthly fathers and could not be called sons of God. Of course, we know that Jesus is *the* Son of God, but this verse is referring to multiple beings that were actually on the earth. They are called sons of God because God created them.

The consensus opinion is that God sent angels to the earth to help man and watch over him. There are several other places in the Bible where God sent angels to the earth, so this instance is consistent with God's behavior. Think about it - Adam and Eve had no parents or schooling, so they needed assistance in learning how to live. There is further confirmation of these angels in the ancient Book of Enoch, a collection of ancient writings that was finished in the second or third century B.C. Even though this book is not in the Bible, it was an important document in Jewish history that reflected several common beliefs. We know of its early existence because it is referred to in the book of Jude in the New Testament and portions of it were discovered in the Dead Sea Scrolls. So, we will view this book as a historical document that may contain errors rather than the inspired Word of God.

The Book of Enoch tells us that about two hundred angels had come to Earth. The book makes it clear that these angels appeared in human form. The angels saw how beautiful the women of Earth were, and they conspired to take them as wives. This of course was a rebellion against God's wishes. According to the Book of Enoch, the angels taught humans many skills. If this is true, it would account for how humans became advanced so quickly.

Some people argue that angels cannot reproduce, but that is not exactly what the Bible says. Instead, the Bible says that they have no need to reproduce. There is no need for angels to reproduce because God created all of the angels and they are eternal spirits. Genesis 6 tells us that these rebel angels reproduced with human wives. Our knowledge of science would indicate that this would be impossible. But, it is recorded in the book of Genesis, which most experts believe was written by Moses. Moses would have been able to verify the story since he met directly with God.

We could speculate that these rebel angels were actually evil humans, or even extraterrestrials from another planet (a popular belief), but the Bible clearly calls them sons of God. Peter confirms that these beings were angels in the New Testament in 2 Peter 2:4, and they are also referenced in Jude 1:6. Therefore, the most likely scenario is that these were angels who rebelled against God. We will see later how God punished these rebels and discuss whether Satan was involved in this rebellion. In any event, the Bible provides documentation that angels existed early in the creation process.

Here is some additional information that we know about angels:

- *Angels are spiritual beings created by God rather than physical beings.* They were created by God in the spiritual dimension and they reside in heaven. There are numerous references in the Bible to the multitudes of angels that live in heaven. We know that God created angels by this verse: "For by him *all* things were created: things in heaven and on earth, visible and invisible, whether thrones or powers or rulers or authorities; all things were created by him and for him." [3] God created angels for his own purposes!

- *There are large numbers of angels.* Hebrews 12:22 tells us that there are "thousands upon thousands" of angels. Deuteronomy 33:2 describes myriads of angels. Revelation 5:11 describes angels in the end times: "Then I looked and heard the voice of many angels, numbering thousands upon thousands, and ten thousand times ten thousand. They encircled the throne and the living creatures and the elders." Ten thousand times ten thousand is one hundred million. It may not be correct to take this literally, but it would be correct to say there is a huge number of angels. It will be an imposing sight when Jesus returns with many of these angels.

- *Angels can appear in human form.* We know this from the passage in Genesis describing angels who rebelled against God. In addition, there is a story in Genesis 18 and 19 where God in the human form of Jesus and two angels appeared to Abraham. Abraham looked up and saw three men. They talked with him, rested, washed their feet, and ate a meal with him. Later the two angels went to Sodom to meet with Lot. While they were in Lot's house, the men of Sodom were banging on the door saying, "Where are the men who came to you tonight? Bring them out to us so that we can have sex with them." [4] These events make it clear that these angels were completely human in their form.

- *Angels are always referred to in masculine form.* Every Bible verse that names an angel or describes an angel refers to them as men.

There are no instances where a female angel is described or named. This alone doesn't mean that they don't exist, but it seems that the Bible would mention them if they existed and were used by God to implement his plans. Most theologians believe that angels are sexless - neither masculine or feminine as we would say in human terms.

- *Angels can travel through the air* Angels can clearly appear wherever they need to. They appear on the ground as normal humans such as the ones who appeared to Abraham and Lot. They have the ability to appear and disappear wherever they choose. Does this mean that angels have wings? In the book of Ezekiel, Ezekiel described a great vision (commonly called "Ezekiel's Wheel"). In this vision, he described cherubim (angels) as having four faces, four wings, and hands like a man's. In Isaiah 6, Isaiah describes seraphim (angels) as having six wings, hands, feet, and a face. In Exodus 25, God tells Moses to make the ark of the covenant with two cherubim images on the top, one at each end, with their wings folded. What we can glean from these verses is that there are at least two different types of angels that have wings. Perhaps some angels have wings and some don't. What is important is that they can travel between Earth and heaven. As far as we know, angels are limited to being in one place at a time, whereas God and the Holy Spirit can be everywhere at the same time.

- *Angels have a free will.* There are several reasons that we know this. First of all, we saw already that a group of angels rebelled against God during the early days of the earth. Peter confirms this by describing their punishment: "God did not spare angels when they sinned, but sent them to hell, putting them into gloomy dungeons to be held for judgment." [5] We also know that Satan was an angel, and that he took one third of all the angels with him when he rebelled against God. This rebellion is described in the book of Revelation: "And there was war in heaven. Michael and his angels fought against the dragon, and the dragon and his angels fought back. But he was not strong enough, and they lost their place in heaven. The great dragon was hurled down—that ancient serpent called the devil, or Satan, who leads the whole world astray. He was hurled to the earth, and his angels with him." [6] Revelation 12:4 tells us (using symbolism) that Satan took one third of the angels with him: "His tail swept a third of the stars out of the sky and flung them to the earth." How could an angel rebel against God unless angels have free will? The angels who are still in heaven with God are there because they *want* to be!

- *Angels can appear selectively.* This means that some angel appearances are seen only by certain people and not by all who are present. This would imply that God is controlling the mind of the viewers as well as the physical appearance of the angels. This happened to Daniel when he met the angel Gabriel: "I, Daniel, was the only one who saw the vision; the men with me did not see it, but such terror overwhelmed them that they fled and hid themselves." [7] In another example, the prophet Elisha found himself surrounded by a large army which wished to kill him. The story continues: "When the servant of the man of God got up and went out early the next morning, an army with horses and chariots had surrounded the city. 'Oh, my lord, what shall we do?' the servant asked. 'Don't be afraid,' the prophet answered. 'Those who are with us are more than those who are with them.' And Elisha prayed, 'O LORD, open his eyes so he may see.' Then the LORD opened the servant's eyes, and he looked and saw the hills full of horses and chariots of fire all around Elisha." [8] The servant could not see the angels until God allowed him to. Perhaps angels are already in our midst and we just don't see them. Maybe we see them only when God reveals them to us. This would certainly be within God's capabilities.

- *We don't always recognize angels who are in our midst.* The Bible tells us that many people have encountered an angel without knowing it. Hebrews 13:2 says: "Do not forget to entertain strangers, for by so doing, some people have entertained angels without knowing it." This tells us that an angel in human form looks and acts just like any human. However, the angels that appeared to the shepherds to announce the birth of Jesus were recognized immediately because the glory of the Lord was shining around them. This tells us that angels can appear either as normal physical beings or as spiritual beings who glorify God.

Angels are spiritual beings, empowered by God to do his work. They have access to God and they can see his glory. It is significant that they serve God because they want to.

What Can Angels Do?

Angels have extensive and supernatural capabilities. This makes sense because God has created and empowered them. Some of these capabilities are outside our knowledge boxes, but totally within God's abilities. We will see below that the Bible has many examples, documented by eyewitnesses, of supernatural events that were caused by angels. Angels are still being used by God today as well.

I vividly remember a time when I should have been killed or seriously injured in a car wreck. I worked in a downtown office building for several years, and after trial and error, I had discovered the best way to get to the parking lot that I used. Every day I took the same route – so often so that it became second nature. One morning, I pulled up to a red light in the downtown area just like I had hundreds of times before. I was the first car in line at the light. I was sitting on a street with tall buildings on my left and right, and I couldn't see anything on the cross street ahead of me other than the traffic light and a few feet on each side of the intersection. My standard procedure was to watch the light and take off just as soon as it changed. On this particular morning, a voice told me to wait a minute after the light changed. It wasn't an audible voice but rather a strong thought that came very clearly into my head. It was the first time anything like this had happened to me. So, I decided to wait for about two or three seconds and then gradually pull out to where I could see if anyone was coming. As soon as I did, a very large truck blew through the intersection trying to beat the red light. It scared me so much that I had to pull over to the side of the road. This truck was coming from the left and would have hit me squarely in the driver's side door if I had left the light when I normally did. The size and speed of the truck would have probably killed me.

I remember thinking about this for a long time. Where did that voice come from? Why did I listen to it? Later in life, I had two other close calls on interstate highways where it was clear that God was watching me and saved me from serious wrecks. These events convinced me that I have a guardian angel. Ever since these close calls, I have been trying to figure out why God saved me. Surely he had something he was saving me for besides being a husband and father. Only recently did I figure out what it was. God knew I was going to write this book. Isn't it great that God looks out for us when we don't realize that we need help? Isn't it great that God has a plan for each of us? The Bible says: "For we are God's workmanship, created in Christ Jesus to do good works, which God prepared in advance for us to do." [9]

Here are some of the capabilities and duties of angels:

- *Angels protect us.* Psalms 91:11-12 says: "For he will command his angels concerning you to guard you in all your ways; they will lift you up in their hands, so that you will not strike your foot against a stone." Do you know what it means when you strike your foot against a stone? It means that you didn't see it coming. These verses are telling us that angels protect us against problems that we aren't even aware of. Yes, we do have guardian angels!

  Many times God sent angels to protect the nation of Israel. For example, 2 Kings 19:35 records the story of a single angel who killed 185 thousand men in the Assyrian camp. Even now, angels are continually battling against Satan on our behalves. Can you imagine how dangerous Satan would be if God did not have his angels restraining him? In the book of Daniel, Daniel describes how he had been waiting on God for an answer, and one day an angel appeared to him. The angel said to Daniel: "Do not be afraid, Daniel. Since the first day that you set your mind to gain understanding and to humble yourself before your God, your words were heard, and I have come in response to them. But the prince of the Persian kingdom resisted me twenty-one days. Then Michael, one of the chief princes, came to help me, because I was detained there with the king of Persia." [10] Most scholars believe that the references to the Persian kingdom refer to a demon (evil spirit). The angel was delayed by twenty one days in reaching Daniel because he was involved in a spiritual warfare battle. The angel was battling the demon because the demon was trying to restrain him.

- *Angels watch over us.* Acts 12 records the story of how an angel freed Peter from prison. The angel entered the prison during the night and woke Peter up. Peter's chains fell off of him, and he and the angel walked right out the entrance without two guards seeing them. Then they came to an iron gate which opened by itself. Shortly after that, the angel disappeared. Peter said "Now I know without a doubt that the Lord sent his angel and rescued me from Herod's clutches and from everything the Jewish people were anticipating." [11]

- *Angels perform miracles and minister to us.* I would say that one angel killing 185 thousand men is a miracle! Hebrews 1:14 says: "Are not all angels ministering spirits sent to serve those who will inherit salvation?" Famous examples of angels ministering include an angel going into a furnace with Shadrach, Meshach and Abednego to protect them from the fire, and an angel protecting Daniel in the lion's den.

- *Angels bring God's message to us.* The angel Gabriel delivered the end times prophecy to Daniel: "While I, Daniel, was watching the vision and trying to understand it, there before me stood one who looked like a man. And I heard a man's voice from the Ulai calling, 'Gabriel, tell this man the meaning of the vision.' As he came near the place where I was standing, I was terrified and fell prostrate. 'Son of man,' he said to me, 'understand that the vision concerns the time of the end.'" [12] Gabriel also told Mary that she would have a son named Jesus who would be from God (Luke 1:26-33).

- *Angels enforce God's judgments and carry out his plan.* An example of this is in 1 Chronicles 21:15: "And God sent an angel to destroy Jerusalem. But as the angel was doing so, the LORD saw it and was grieved because of the calamity and said to the angel who was destroying the people, 'Enough! Withdraw your hand.'" God also tells us that his angels will deliver judgment in the end times: "The Son of Man will send out his angels, and they will weed out of his kingdom everything that causes sin and all who do evil. They will throw them into the fiery furnace, where there will be weeping and gnashing of teeth." [13]

- *Angels can communicate with God.* We know that children have angels who have direct access to God. Jesus says: "See that you do not look down on one of these little ones. For I tell you that their angels in heaven always see the face of my Father in heaven." [14] Of course, communication with God is essential if angels are to do God's work and to deliver his message to us.

- *Angels live forever.* The only angels who are not eternally in heaven are the ones who rejected God and became fallen angels. These angels are still eternal beings, but they will be judged and condemned to eternal damnation during the end times. There is no provision for salvation for angels who reject God because Jesus did not die for them. Those angels who have served God faithfully will live forever with God in heaven.

- *Angels have assigned tasks.* As discussed previously, children have their own angels. We have guardian angels. Michael is the angel for Israel, and he wages continual war against Satan. Gabriel brings God's messages to Earth. Heaven appears to be a very organized place, which is exactly what we would expect.

God's angels play a key role in executing his plan for us. The angels were created by God to be eternal spiritual beings who help God implement his plan. Angels are not a form of God, but they are creations of God. Popular beliefs that we can become an angel when we die or that we should worship angels or pray to angels are just not supported in the Bible. Our focus should always be on worshipping God (the Creator) rather than any of his creations.

Summary

Here are some things we learned about angels in this chapter:

- Angels are spiritual beings who were created by God to do his work.
- There are large numbers of angels (well into the millions).
- Angels can appear to us in human form and behave just like humans.
- Angels can appear and disappear instantly and selectively.
- Angels can travel between heaven and Earth.
- Angels have a free will; they serve God because they want to.
- Satan and his demons are fallen angels who will be condemned by God in the end times.
- Angels protect us, minister to us, watch over us, and bring God's message to us.
- Some angels are continually waging war with Satan.
- Angels deliver God's judgment, including end times judgments.

CHAPTER 7:

Is Satan Real?

Many people do not like to talk about Satan, demons, or fallen angels. I can understand why! They are evil, destructive creatures. Perhaps you would rather just ignore them or pretend that they don't exist. If you do, you will be ignoring the truth. These beings are your enemy, and they are attacking your mind whether you realize it or not. It would be wise to know and recognize your enemy and make sure you are filled with the Holy Spirit to help you resist these attacks.

One of my favorite television shows in the early 1970's was *The Flip Wilson Show*. Flip Wilson was a comedian who invented several characters that he played on the show, including the sassy woman Geraldine Jones, and Reverend Leroy (minister of the Church of What's Happening Now). Geraldine was always getting into trouble and saying or doing things that she shouldn't. Each time she would get caught, she would say in her most sassy voice, "The devil made me do it!" This became a popular phrase in America during that time, both as a joke and somewhat as an excuse that people would use.

Of course, this phrase goes all the way back to Adam and Eve. Eve used this excuse when God asked her why she had eaten the forbidden fruit. And what did Adam say? He blamed it on Eve! Isn't it interesting that so many people today think their problems are always someone else's fault? Eve and Geraldine Jones are not correct. The devil can't *make* us do things. Instead, he tempts us by making things attractive to us, deceiving us, and lying. We still have free will to listen to him or not. Looking at this another way is that the devil's only power over us is what we allow him to have! I find it very comforting to know that Satan and the evil spirits have *no* power over us. When we sin, we are *always* responsible because our actions reflect our own free will. Maybe you don't want to be accountable, but you are.

As we saw earlier, a recent Barna survey revealed that most Americans don't believe that Satan is real or that we are born as sinners.[1] Perhaps these beliefs are a big factor in why so many people think they can go to heaven just by being a good person. I believe Satan is a real being, and we are his targets. The statistics show that Satan is making a big impact. People are leaving Christianity and looking elsewhere for their spirituality, or just avoiding organized religion completely. Let's look at who Satan is and how he is making an impact.

Who Is Satan?

Satan is an angel who rebelled against God. This obviously proves that angels have a free will. Satan was one of the most magnificent of all God's angels. He held a very responsible position in heaven as a cherub who guarded the throne of God. He was an angel who was highly trusted and admired by God. God describes Satan as a fallen angel in the following verses from the book of Ezekiel. Although this passage is also directed at the King of Tyre, most scholars agree that God is describing Satan:

> "You were the model of perfection, full of wisdom and perfect in beauty. You were in Eden, the garden of God; every precious stone adorned you: ruby, topaz and emerald, chrysolite, onyx and jasper, sapphire, turquoise and beryl. Your settings and mountings were made of gold; on the day you were created they were prepared. You were anointed as a guardian cherub, for so I ordained you. You were on the holy mount of God; you walked among the fiery stones. You were blameless in your ways from the day you were created till wickedness was found in you. Through your widespread trade you were filled with violence, and you sinned. So I drove you in disgrace from the mount of God, and I expelled you, O guardian cherub, from among the fiery stones. Your heart became proud on account

of your beauty, and you corrupted your wisdom because of your splendor. So I threw you to the earth; I made a spectacle of you before kings." [2]

This passage shows that Satan was one of the most impressive angels that God created. He was beautiful to look at and full of wisdom. God rewarded him by making him a guardian cherub. But Satan sinned against God. God makes it clear in these verses that Satan's pride caused his demise. He was proud of his looks, but this pride corrupted his wisdom. These things caused him to think he was equal to God and he wanted the additional glory.

Because Satan is a fallen angel, he is member of the spirit world. We can think of him as an evil spirit. In fact, he is the most evil of all the evil spirits and seems to have great influence over other evil spirits.

Satan is currently being restrained by God. Satan was described by Billy Graham as "an angel on a leash". This is a pretty good description, because Satan can only do what God allows him to do. Earlier we read the story in Daniel 10 where an angel apologized for the delay in reaching Daniel because of a battle he had to fight against a demon. Satan and his followers are waging continual war against us and against God. Satan wins a few battles here and there (mostly because we allow him to), but God will not allow him to win the war. It is hard to imagine how difficult life would be if Satan were not being restrained to some extent.

It is significant to note that Satan and Jesus were in heaven at the same time. Jesus said, "I tell you the truth," Jesus answered, "before Abraham was born, I am!" [3] Jesus was making it clear that he existed in heaven before he came to Earth. He existed during the time of creation and prior to the time Satan was thrown to the earth. Satan is well acquainted with Jesus and who he is. Jesus is the enemy of Satan just as much as God himself. We need to acknowledge that knowing who Jesus is just isn't the same as worshipping him. Even Satan knows that Jesus is the Son of God, but he does not worship him.

We see in the Bible that Satan began his attacks on Jesus just as soon as

Jesus was born. In Matthew 2, we see that the Magi (commonly referred to as "wise men") were supposed to report back to Herod when they found the newborn baby Jesus. However, they took another route home and did not report to him. "When Herod realized that he had been outwitted by the Magi, he was furious, and he gave orders to kill all the boys in Bethlehem and its vicinity who were two years old and under, in accordance with the time he had learned from the Magi." [4] Joseph, Mary, and Jesus fled to Egypt after an angel warned them about what Herod was going to do. Do you think Satan may have influenced the mind of Herod? I do. What kind of person could kill innocent children without being under the influence of Satan?

Have you ever wondered what Satan looks like? When I was growing up, Satan was always pictured in human form with two horns, a tail, and a mean looking face that often had a goatee. These images are burned into my mind, and even today people who have goatees remind me of these images. (I also have a picture of myself when I was around six years old in a Halloween costume that looks like the devil I just described.) Perhaps Satan was thought to be red because people believed that he was living in hell and it was a pretty hot place. Perhaps people thought he was red because he was so mad at God. I don't really know where these images came from, but they are not biblical. Satan will end up in hell, but he is not there right now. He is roaming the earth and the heavens trying to deceive us. As we just read in the book of Ezekiel, Satan was probably the most beautiful angel in heaven. He is a liar who is cunning and deceptive, and as we saw, he is extremely proud of himself. If Satan appeared in human form, he would probably be very attractive.

Satan's attractiveness makes him even more dangerous. The Bible confirms Satan's attractive appearance in these verses that talk about false prophets: "...Satan himself masquerades as an angel of light. It is not surprising, then, if his servants masquerade as servants of righteousness." [5] An angel of light would be an angel sent from God. We also see that Satan himself is a masquerader. This makes him even more difficult to recognize.

One of the most important things that we know about Satan is that he is a liar. Jesus makes this clear in John 8:44 when describing Satan: "He was a murderer from the beginning, not holding to the truth, for there is no truth in him. When he lies, he speaks his native language, for he is a liar and the father of lies." This verse provides clear evidence that Satan is a being that exists, that he is a murderer, and a liar. We know that Jesus is well acquainted with Satan. We know that Jesus said these words because they were written down by an eyewitness. We know that Jesus cannot lie because he is God in human form. It is hard to defend the position of some modern experts who say there is no such thing as Satan or sin. Satan lies to us, and he is really good at it. He lies about God in hopes that we will turn somewhere else. As we will see later, he has contradicted every major point in the Bible including predictions about the end times. Many of his lies are delivered through humans who are masquerading as servants of righteousness. Some of his victims are those who think he doesn't exist. It takes a really good liar to convince someone that you don't exist!

Satan started his mission by attacking Eve in the Garden of Eden. There is no reason to believe he has given up over the last several thousand years. There is no doubt that he has influenced many people and many cultures during this period, and he continues to do this today.

What is Satan's Agenda?

Satan's agenda is very clear. He wants to replace God in the organization chart of the universe. Have you ever worked with anyone who was so ambitious that he didn't care who he stepped on to get ahead? People like this will break the rules, stab you in the back, create vicious gossip, and often come across as being extremely arrogant. They are dangerous because they will act like they are trying to help their employer but are really implementing their own agenda. Everything they do is pointed to their own personal glorification. These people are some of the most obnoxious people that you will ever run across. But Satan is worse.

Satan's agenda is confirmed in the book of Isaiah in a message that God gave to Isaiah. God is addressing this message to the King of Babylon, who at that time was the embodiment of evil. In reality, he is describing Satan in these verses:

> "You said in your heart, 'I will ascend to heaven; I will raise my throne above the stars of God; I will sit enthroned on the mount of assembly, on the utmost heights of the sacred mountain. I will ascend above the tops of the clouds; I will make myself like the Most High.'" [6]

How can Satan accomplish this objective? Here are the steps he is taking:

- He needs to defeat God's angels, which he is trying to do.
- He needs to keep as many of us out of heaven as possible, which he is trying to do.
- He needs to discredit God so that no one would want to worship him, which he is trying to do.
- He needs to declare himself equal to God, which he will do through the Antichrist during the end times.

This is a strategic plan that is doomed for failure. The implementation of this plan is called spiritual warfare, and this warfare is going on right now. Fortunately, God has given each of us free will so that we can choose which side to align with. We cannot remain neutral in this battle! If we don't align with God, it means by default that we have aligned with Satan.

How do we know that Satan is doomed for failure? We know because God says so, and God sees the future. During the end times, Satan will be defeated by Jesus and sent to his permanent place in hell as stated in Revelation 20:10: "And the devil, who deceived them, was thrown into the lake of burning sulfur, where the beast and the false prophet had been thrown. They will be tormented day and night forever and ever." The lake of burning sulfur is hell. Satan and all the evil spirits will be there forever, as will those who don't have Jesus as their Savior. Does this sound like a place where you would like to spend eternity, with no chance of ever getting out?

I believe that Satan, a fallen angel, realizes that his time is limited. There are a couple of Bible verses that would indicate this. The first is when Jesus drove some demons out of two men. Upon seeing Jesus, the demons said, "'What do you want with us, Son of God?' they shouted. 'Have you come here to torture us before the appointed time?'" [7] This is a fascinating story. First of all, the demons recognized Jesus and acknowledged that he was the Son of God. Second, they knew that it wasn't their time yet (meaning their time to be condemned to hell).

In Revelation, we see that Satan and his angels are thrown down to the earth. God issues this warning: "But woe to the earth and the sea, because the devil has gone down to you! He is filled with fury, because he knows that his time is short." [8] Satan is working with a sense of urgency because he knows that his time is short. He wants to do as much damage as possible in the time he has left! Many people do not feel a sense of urgency to get right with God. They seem to be able to ignore some of the most important tasks that they have in life. They are too involved in self-satisfaction and the pursuit of happiness to realize that our existence after we die will last much longer than our time on Earth. If you have not reconciled with God, you are helping Satan accomplish his objectives. Please don't put this off.

How Does Satan Work?

What are some of the ways that Satan implements his agenda? We have already talked about lying, which is Satan's core strategy. Satan uses lies to help deceive us, and he deceives us by making things appeal to us. Sometimes, these are physical things and sometimes they are things that relate to the mind. For example, pride makes us emulate Satan.

Satan's temptations hit us in our weak spots. Satan tempted Jesus after Jesus was baptized and had spent forty days in the wilderness. Jesus had fasted for forty days, and he would have been hungry and tired when Satan appeared to him. Satan said "If you are the Son of God, tell these stones to become bread." [9] Jesus was able to resist this temptation, and two others that Satan offered to him. Don't you think it is interesting that Satan hits us in our weakest spots and our weakness moments? When you are tempted, doesn't it seem to be in places where you have the least resistance? Jesus was hungry and weak, and Satan offered him food.

Many of Satan's temptations start with the word "if." For example, he told Eve that if she ate the forbidden fruit, she would surely not die. Why would Satan say to Jesus: "If you are the Son of God?" He knew already that Jesus was the Son of God! He was testing Jesus to see if he had a weakness. He was trying to bring Jesus down to his level. After three of Satan's unsuccessful attempts, Jesus just told him to leave and he did (Matthew 4:10). Luke's account of this story says: "When the devil had finished all this tempting, he left him until an opportune time." [10]

Another strategy Satan uses is to attack us when we receive the Word of God. Jesus tells a parable about a farmer who was sowing seed. Some of the seed fell on a path, was trampled, and eaten by birds. When explaining this parable to the disciples, Jesus said "This is the meaning of the parable: The seed is the word of God. Those along the path are the ones who hear, and then the devil comes and takes away the word from their hearts, so that they may not believe and be saved." [11] Satan does not want us to hear God's message, so he will try to distract us or find other things for us to focus on rather than God. I believe that Satan turns up the heat on us when we start getting closer to God. In my life, the financial difficulties of my business started while I was teaching a youth group in church, which was one of the most satisfying and happy times in my life.

If we have difficulties in our lives, we should look at the possibility that Satan is causing them. We should think about whether these difficulties are moving us away from God. Finally, we should ask God to use these times to strengthen us.

One of the greatest stories in the Bible is the story of Joseph. Joseph was a son of Jacob, who later was renamed Israel. God had great plans for Joseph – he was going to make him ruler over all of Egypt and allow him to save his family (the descendants of Israel) from a great famine. Joseph was favored both by God and his father. So, what happened to him? His brothers became jealous and sold him into slavery. How did God use this? He saw that Joseph became a trusted employee in the house of one of Egypt's most wealthy people. Then, Satan had the wealthy Egyptian's wife accuse Joseph of something he didn't do, and Joseph was thrown into jail. How did God use this? Joseph was put in charge of the prison. Later, two of the pharaoh's associates were thrown into prison for a time while Joseph was there, and Joseph was able to interpret dreams for them. Two years later, the pharaoh needed someone to interpret a dream, and one of the associates remembered Joseph. He was the only one able to interpret the pharaoh's dream, which saved Egypt from a great famine. Joseph was then put in charge of the pharaoh's palace, according to God's plan.

Through this entire story, God's plan for Joseph did not change. In retrospect, it appears that some of the difficulties that Joseph had were necessary in order for God to get him into the pharaoh's palace. Sometimes, God takes bad things (or things that we interpret to be bad) that happen to us and uses them to our advantage. Romans 8:28 says "And we know that in all things God works for the good of those who love him, who have been called according to his purpose."

Satan tries to implement his agenda by influencing your spirit and your mind. The spiritual portion of your body is filled by whatever you choose. We know from the Bible that Satan's demons can possess a human. Satan himself can influence your spirit if you let him. A good example of this is the actions of the disciple Judas, who betrayed Jesus. The Bible says: "The evening meal was being served, and the devil had already prompted Judas Iscariot, son of Simon, to betray Jesus." [12] Some people think that Judas and Jesus had arranged this earlier, because Jesus knew that someone needed to betray him. This is ridiculous! Jesus did not need to be betrayed. Everyone knew who he was and what he had said and done. The idea that Judas was needed to point out who Jesus was just doesn't make sense. The point made by John in this verse is that Satan influenced Judas. Later in the evening meal, Jesus gave Judas a piece of bread to signify that he knew who the betrayer was. "As soon as Judas took the bread, Satan entered into him." [13] Jesus knew all along that Judas would betray him because he knew Judas' heart and how he would react to Satan's temptations.

Finally, let's look at Satan's capabilities. Since Satan is a fallen angel, we must assume that he was created the same as any other angel. He is a spirit, just like the other angels. There is no mention in the Bible that God took away the capabilities that Satan had as an angel because of his rebellion. If Satan and the rebellious angels that are with him retained their previous capabilities, then they are able to appear in human form, appear and disappear instantly, travel throughout the earth and the heavens, and influence us just like good angels do. We also see in the study of Revelation that Satan will be allowed to perform miracles in the end times. These supernatural acts will confuse many people and cause them to move away from the one true God.

Regardless of what Satan's powers and capabilities are, we need to focus on what I said in the first part of this chapter – Satan cannot *make* us do anything! He can only tempt us. These temptations are often strong and attractive, and it is hard to deal with them on our own. We can ask for God's help in resisting these temptations and forgiving us when our sin nature gets the best of us.

Where is Satan?

It is pretty clear in the Bible that Satan is on the Earth. There is some debate about when Satan appeared and whether he still has access to heaven, which we will cover in this section.

We can tell that Satan existed on Earth during the time of Adam and Eve because the Bible makes it clear that Satan is the one who tempted Eve. This event marked the beginning of the Original Sin that we are all born with today. We are not exactly sure when Satan rebelled against God, but we know that some sort of rebellion took place because Satan was not on Earth doing God's work. In fact, he was doing the opposite. He decided to target God's creations as a way of getting back at God.

The Bible tells us that Satan has lots of help! In Revelation 12, we are told that Satan got into a great war with Michael and his angels, and that Satan and his angels were thrown to Earth. The implication in Revelation 12 is that Satan's angels could have been one third of the angels in heaven. Based on numbers we looked at earlier, this would represent millions of fallen angels. Has this event already happened or is it happening in the future?

It is not my intent to analyze in detail all of the symbolism in the book of Revelation. There are plenty of books you can read to get more information. I think it is clear that Satan and his rebellious angels would have been on Earth during the time of Jesus, and they are still among us today.

The Bible also supports the theory that Satan still has access to God for the purpose of accusing us. In Revelation 12:10, Satan is referred to as the "accuser of our brothers and sisters." In fact, the word for Satan in Hebrew means "accuser." Think about this for a minute. If you had to go to court for some reason, you would probably hire a good lawyer to represent yourself. When you appear before God in heaven, the Bible tells us that Satan is the accuser (prosecutor) and Jesus is the judge, jury, and defense attorney. If we haven't arranged for Jesus to be our defense attorney, then we will not have one. We will be pronounced guilty based on the fact that our names are not recorded in the *Book of Life* (the term used in the Bible to denote those who have accepted Jesus).

We also know that Satan has access to God based on a story in the book of Job. "One day the angels came to present themselves before the LORD, and Satan also came with them. The LORD said to Satan, 'Where have you come from?' Satan answered the LORD, 'From roaming through the earth and going back and forth in it.'" [14] Of course God knew where Satan had been. What he really wanted to know was why Satan was in front of him. Satan was there because he wanted permission to tempt Job.

We also see Satan as an accuser in Zechariah 3:1: "Then he showed me Joshua the high priest standing before the angel of the LORD, and Satan standing at his right side to accuse him."

Satan is here on Earth looking for opportunities to accuse us before God. If you think this is disturbing, then have you lined up your defense attorney?

What Are Fallen Angels?

In actuality, all of the angels who followed Satan are fallen angels. They are now operating as evil spirits in the world. There are a few places in the Bible where the text refers to fallen angels who were locked up by God in the earth. What did these angels do that caused them to be locked up? Where are they now? In 2 Peter 2:4, Peter says: "...God did not spare angels when they sinned, but sent them to hell [the Abyss], putting them into gloomy dungeons to be held for judgment." Peter is referring to something that happened in the past. He is not referring to the one third of angels who rebelled with Satan, because Satan and those angels have not been confined to hell yet. Which angels is Peter talking about? Why are these angels being held for judgment?

Genesis Account

To get the answer to these questions, we need to go back to Genesis and the time of Noah. Some verses in Genesis that we looked at earlier give us these answers:

> "When men began to increase in number on the earth and daughters were born to them, the sons of God saw that the daughters of men were beautiful, and they married any of them they chose. Then the LORD said, "My Spirit will not contend with man forever, for he is mortal; his days will be a hundred and twenty years." The Nephilim were on the earth in those days—and also afterward—when the sons of God went to the daughters of men and had children by them. They were the heroes of old, men of renown. The LORD saw how great man's wickedness on the earth had become, and that every inclination of the thoughts of his heart was only evil all the time. The LORD was grieved that he had made man on the earth, and his heart was filled with pain." [15]

As we discussed earlier, the sons of God referred to in this passage were most likely angels. These angels did not rebel specifically against God, but instead they chose to sin. They lusted after the women on Earth ("daughters of men"), and the Bible says they married any that they chose. This implies that the marriages were forceful. When the angels and their earthly wives had children, they were called Nephilim. There is some debate about the exact translation of the original Hebrew for Nephilim, but there is no debate that the Nephilim were giants ("men of renown").

The Nephilim were cross-breeds. They corrupted the bloodline of Adam and Eve. The fact that angels in human form had children with human wives was totally outside God's plan and therefore was sinful. We don't know whether Satan tempted these angels, but he was in the area and there is a good chance that he was involved. The Nephilim helped to create an extremely corrupt Earth – so much so that God was "grieved that he had made man" as described in Genesis 6.

God's solution was to create a flood to wipe out the evil on Earth. Noah and his family were spared because Noah was a righteous man who was not part of the corrupted bloodline.

As pointed out by Missler and Eastman in their book *Alien Encounters*, there were four groups who were dealt with during the flood. One group, Noah and his family, was saved. Another group consisted solely of Enoch, who was evacuated and taken to heaven before the flood. The third and largest group, which included everyone other than Noah's family, perished in the flood. The fourth group consisted of the fallen angels who were locked up in the earth to wait for final judgment at the end times. Later, we will see parallels between the end times scenarios and the time of Noah.

The Book of Jude confirms that the fallen angels were locked up until their final judgment day, which will occur during the end times. Satan was not locked up in the earth at this time based on the fact that Satan appears in the Bible numerous times after the flood.

Enoch Account

The Book of Enoch was an important Jewish historical document in the two centuries prior to the birth of Jesus but is not part of our modern Bible.

My curiosity got the best of me, so I read the only translation of Enoch that I could find, which is basically in King James English.

There are a lot of things in this book that are consistent with the Bible but also errors and things that are not consistent with the Bible. In addition, the book may have been written by several authors over hundreds of years, which causes questions about its credibility. Even so, it was widely known to Jews who lived in the time of Christ and was referred to in the New Testament book of Jude. So, we should treat this book as a Jewish historical document and not part of the inspired Word of God.

The Book of Enoch provides more details than the book of Genesis about the fallen angels. Enoch calls them "Watchers" because they were God's representatives who were to watch over God's creation. According to the Enoch account, the leaders of the fallen angels came to Enoch after God discovered their sin and asked for Enoch to plead with God on their behalf. Enoch did this and received an answer from God, which was that the fallen angels would have no peace. The Bible does not confirm the details in the Book of Enoch, but it does confirm that the fallen angels are now locked up awaiting their final judgment day during the end times. We know this from reading Jude 1:6.

What Are Demons?

We know that Satan and the angels that rebelled with him are evil spirits who are roaming the earth (except for the ones who were locked up by God). Because they are angels, they can move around freely, appear as humans, disappear, and influence our behavior. So, what are demons and where did they come from? Surely God did not create them on purpose.

Most scholars believe that demons are fallen angels. God did not create demons; he created angels with a free will who decided to reject him. There are several theories about which fallen angels became demons. One theory is that *all* of the rebellious angels (evil spirits) are now demons. In fact, the term *demon* may be just another term for fallen angel. The problem with this theory is that encounters with demons in the Bible occur when those demons have inhabited human bodies. The Bible says that angels can appear as humans but doesn't mention examples where an angel inhabited a human's body. Another theory is that demons are the fallen angels who have been locked up in the earth to wait for their final judgment, which is eternal damnation. However, the Bible tells us that they will be locked up until the end times, so we know that they are not roaming the earth. A third theory is that demons are the spirits of the Nephilim (the offspring) themselves. Supporters of this theory believe that the Nephilim physically died, but that their spirits had nowhere to go because of the way they were created. The Bible does not directly tell us where demons came from, but it confirms in several places that they exist. Regardless of how demons were created, it is clear that demons are on "the dark side."

As Christians, we shouldn't really care where demons come from. We simply need to acknowledge that they exist and learn how to avoid them.

Demons have a unique problem that is not shared by other evil spirits. That problem is that they seem to need to find a body to possess. Demon possession is another phenomenon that you might not believe in, but it is real. Jesus drove out demons on many occasions in front of hundreds of witnesses. Even today, we still have exorcisms occurring. They don't receive as much publicity as they used to, but they are real. The movie *The Exorcist* was based on a real life situation.

I realize that many people just don't believe in demons, demon possession, evil spirits, ghosts, and other unexplained paranormal activity. I would rather say that we just don't understand things like this. Demons are described in the Bible in several places that we will look at, and I believe the Bible is true.

Let's look at some of the Bible's information on demons:

- Demons cause significant problems in humans. Jesus encountered violent demons in this passage that we read earlier: "When he arrived at the other side in the region of the Gadarenes, two demon-possessed men coming from the tombs met him. They were so violent that no one could pass that way." [16] Demons possess not only your mind, but they can take control of your body. When you become a Christian, you are filled with the Holy Spirit, which prevents demon possession.

- Demons are subject to Jesus. The Bible describes one of Jesus' encounters with demons: "That evening after sunset the people brought to Jesus all the sick and demon-possessed. The whole town gathered at the door, and Jesus healed many who had various diseases. He also drove out many demons, but he would not let the demons speak because they knew who he was." [17] First of all, we notice that the demons leave the body when Jesus commands them to leave. Second, they obey him when he tells them not to speak. Third, we can see that the demons know Jesus and recognize his authority. This might indicate that demons are spirits who formerly lived in heaven.

- Demons can possess animals. Jesus was driving some demons out of a man, as described in Luke: "And they [the demons] begged him repeatedly not to order them to go into the Abyss. A large herd of pigs was feeding there on the hillside. The demons begged Jesus to let them go into them, and he gave them permission. When the demons came out of the man, they went into the pigs, and the herd rushed down the steep bank into the lake and was drowned." [18] In one of the more interesting stories in the Bible, the demons begged Jesus to let them go into animals. But, even more interesting is that the demons begged Jesus to not send them into the Abyss. This is the place where the fallen angels have been locked up since the time of Noah.

- Demons know their fate. In the same story we looked at earlier, the demons asked Jesus: "'What do you want with us, Son of God?' they shouted. 'Have you come here to torture us before the appointed time?'" [19] We looked at this verse earlier in this chapter because it points out that the demons realize they are doomed at some point in the future.

- Demons have a role in the end times. In Revelation 16:14, we see that Satan will use demons to gather the nations of the world together for battle against God: "They are spirits of demons performing miraculous signs, and they go out to the kings of the whole world, to gather them for the battle on the great day of God Almighty." The fact that these evil demons will be allowed to perform miraculous signs will deceive many people.

Demons and fallen angels, including Satan, will be condemned to hell for eternity. God has not provided for salvation for angels. They are not human and were not born with Original Sin. They were born with eternal life, unlike humans. When an angel rejects God, they are judged immediately without provision for forgiveness.

Is Satan Behind the New Age?

Before I wrote this book, my image of the New Age was based on hippies who were into crystals, astrology, transcendental meditation, and "The Age of Aquarius". After additional research, I discovered that there is more. Many of the concepts we have discussed already can be associated with New Age thinking. These include universalism (all ways lead to whatever you call god), relativism (there is no such thing as absolute truth), and pantheism (god is not a personal being but is in everything in nature). I wondered where these beliefs came from, so I did more research. The results were surprising.

What I discovered was that many of these beliefs have originated or been refined by channelers. A channeler is basically someone who believes that they are receiving messages from ETs in other solar systems who are more advanced than we are. Substantially all of these messages deal with spiritual and religious matters, and many of them are found in New Age thinking today. *These messages are clearly contrary to the Bible.* If aliens are real and they are advanced beings from other planets, then why are they talking to us about spiritual issues? Why don't they tell us how to cure the common cold or share more practical knowledge with us? I have serious doubts about whether these aliens exist, but look at what Americans believe based on a combination of several surveys about the alien phenomenon:

- About three fourths believe in life on other planets.
- Over 80 million believe that we have been visited by extraterrestrials.
- Almost half of the population believe UFOs are real.
- Over 60 percent believe that UFOs contain ETs from other planets.
- Roughly 15 percent say that they have seen a UFO.
- 80 percent believe that the government is withholding information about UFOs and ETs.
- About half believe that aliens have abducted humans.
- About three fourths believe in at least one form of paranormal activity (ESP, ghosts, communicating with the dead, etc.)

A 2012 Pew Forum survey reveals that approximately one-fourth of Americans (both religious and non-religious) believe in spiritual energy in physical things (like mountains, trees, etc.), believe in astrology, reincarnation, and yoga as a spiritual exercise.[20]

Why is it that so many people can believe in something that has no evidence or support, yet so many do not believe that Jesus is the Son of God in spite of eyewitness accounts and credible written and historical evidence? Is it possible that some people are believing only what they want to believe without considering the evidence available?

The Spirituality of Aliens

I am going to assume that these alleged aliens, if they do exist, are actually members of the spirit world because of the spiritual nature of their messages. Therefore, we need to determine whether they are good or evil spirits. If these aliens are from the spirit world, then it is impossible to build a case that they were sent by God. God does not need to give us spiritual messages through aliens, because he already told us everything we need to know in the Bible. Current communications with God come through the Holy Spirit or God's angels, not through any other type of spirit.

I spent some time reading the alien spiritual messages to see if they would help us identify the true source. What I learned is that there are some consistent patterns in what they are saying:

- Many alien groups take credit for creating the world, populating it, and helping early men learn various technologies. They deny that God had anything to do with creation.
- There is not a single group that acknowledges that Jesus is the Son of God. In fact, there are so many false statements about who he is that they actually contradict each other.
- Many groups claim that Jesus did not die on the cross.
- Several groups spend a lot of time talking about the end times. Of course, they have a little different spin on what is going to happen. They view this as a time of peace and prosperity, with a single worldwide government. They view the removal of Christians from the Earth as a good thing for those who are left behind.
- Several groups deny that God is a separate being. Instead they say that God is in everything, including us, and everything is God. The way to find God is to improve your consciousness.
- Many groups thinks that Gaia (Mother Earth) has an emotional and spiritual body and a conscious will.

There is more, but don't waste your time looking for it. The fact that these statements contradict the Bible is proof of their falsehood. Not only that, but these messages contradict each other in many cases. Furthermore, why would anyone believe that an alien has knowledge about the future?

There is no logical basis for saying that these messages are from God. Everything in the universe is either good or evil. God tells us that if we are not *for* him, then we must be against him (Matthew 12:30). The reality is that these alleged aliens don't support God's agenda. These aliens are not God's messengers, and it is hard to come up with any valid reasons why we should believe *anything* they are saying (if they really exist).

None of the alleged aliens profess that Jesus Christ is the Son of God. This is the ultimate test that we can apply to determine whether these aliens or spirits can be trusted. This test is described in the Bible:

"This is how you can recognize the Spirit of God: Every spirit that acknowledges that Jesus Christ has come in the flesh is from God, but every spirit that does not acknowledge Jesus is not from God. This is the spirit of the antichrist, which you have heard is coming and even now is already in the world." [21]

The aliens do not pass this test because they do not acknowledge publically that Jesus is the Son of God (even though they know this to be true). In fact, these verses tell us specifically that these aliens are spirits of the antichrist (Satan). There are millions of good spirits in the universe – they are called angels. They do their work silently. They are not involved in channeling, and they certainly don't contradict God's Word. They protect us from evil spirits when we don't realize it. In the meantime, we see testimony about evil spirits or aliens flying around in our skies, allegedly abducting humans, and pushing an agenda that is designed to pull people away from God. Is it just a coincidence that Satan's agenda is to pull people away from God? I doubt it.

If you don't think these theories are mainstream, you are wrong. A lot of these theories have made their way into popular television shows, and some of our famous channelers have been given time on national television as well. There are also New Age so-called churches that try to look like Christian churches that are attracting people from all religions. Satan's efforts to deceive us are widespread! So if you have bought in to any of these theories, you are leaning on something that is not stable.

I believe that we can conclude three things after examining the evidence:

1. The alien agenda is consistent with Satan's agenda.
2. The alien agenda is consistent with the New Age agenda.
3. The New Age agenda is consistent with Satan's agenda.

Until the final judgment occurs, Satan and other evil spirits are roaming the earth spreading evil and trying to pull us away from God. You don't need to look too hard to see some of the results of their work. After reading all the evidence, are you still convinced that Satan is not real? Have you thought about the forces of evil when you are deciding what to believe about God? Do you realize that Satan, the fallen angels, and the demons are trying to keep you from accepting Jesus as your savior? Do you realize that Jesus is the only way you can defeat these evil forces?

Summary

Here are the major points of this chapter:

- Satan is a fallen angel who rejected God because of his pride and ego.
- Satan is roaming the earth and is currently restrained by God.
- Satan is a liar who makes things attractive to us.
- Satan wants to replace God by destroying his angels and followers.
- Satan has deceived one third of the angels in heaven who have become his followers. These angels are now evil spirits.
- The rebellious angels have the same capabilities as other angels – they can appear as human, disappear, move from one place to another, and influence our thoughts.
- Satan accuses us before God; Jesus will defend us if we trust in him.
- Demons are evil spirits who can physically possess people and animals.
- Demons, evil spirits, and Satan are as real today as in the time of Jesus.
- New Age beliefs contradict the Bible and are being used by Satan to turn people away from God.
- Demons, evil spirits, and Satan acknowledge that Jesus is the Son of God; there is a big difference between acknowledging that Jesus is the Son of God and worshiping him.

CHAPTER 8:

Spiritual Warfare

A few years ago, Jim Carrey starred in the movie *Liar Liar*. He played a lawyer who was a habitual liar but was forced to tell the truth for twenty-four hours after his son made a birthday wish. If you have seen this movie, you know that it is one of Jim Carrey's funniest movies. Some of the lines he delivers when telling the truth are classics. The saying "the truth hurts" is shown to be true when he tells people things that would normally not be considered tactful. Being tactful is not always lying, and it is appropriate in many cases. On the other hand, lying can be very harmful, and this movie does a good job of showing the damaged relationships that occurred because of the constant lying that took place between a lawyer and his family.

We have already learned in this book that Satan is the most dangerous liar in the universe. In this chapter, we will look at some of Satan's lies and deceptions that are intended to pull us away from God. Let's recap what we have learned about Satan so far:

- Jesus said that when Satan lies, he is speaking his native language and that there is no truth in him. What if God put Satan on a witness stand and forced him to tell the truth for 24 hours? That would really be interesting.
- Satan is the spiritual being who makes bad things attractive to us.
- Satan is the being who creates doubts about God and what God says in the Bible.
- Satan is behind many of the religious beliefs that are keeping people away from God.

- Satan is the being who has no conscience, no morals, and no respect for anything.
- Satan's mission is to defeat God, and he doesn't care who he destroys along the way. Lying is his weapon, and humans are his victims. He started his lying in the Garden of Eden, and it is still going on today.
- Satan accuses us before God. It is not very comforting to know that a being who cannot tell the truth is accusing us before God.

Satan has a consistent strategy of trying to discredit everything that God ever did or will do in the future. Here are some of his biggest lies and deceptions:

- He contradicts statements in the Bible or spins them into different meanings.
- He reduces God's miracles to events that either didn't happen or counterfeits them with his own version.
- He reduces God's majesty by convincing us that God is within us and we can all become gods.
- He tempts us to rely on ourselves by saying that there is no such thing as sin or that we are not born with a sinful nature.
- He tells us that Jesus is not the Son of God and that Jesus is not the only way to God.
- He tells us that we can get to heaven by just being a good person.
- He tells us that the Christian church is no longer relevant and that we should look elsewhere for our religion.
- He appeals to our desires for self-control and getting exactly what we want by telling us that we can engage in cafeteria religion and still be reconciled to God.
- He convinces us that we need to change our beliefs by saying that change is good and necessary.

He makes these lies attractive by taking advantage of some of our human weaknesses.

The volume of these lies and the number of different sources that they come from make it difficult for many people to identify the truth. Who are you supposed to believe when two people make conflicting statements? I am sure you have all seen courtroom dramas on television or in a movie where the final guilt or innocence of the accused is determined only by testimony of the witnesses that were called. This creates the "he said, she said" scenario where witnesses often give conflicting testimony. How is the jury supposed to decide who to believe if there is no evidence to support any of the testimony? We know that God cannot lie and Satan cannot tell the truth, but Satan is an expert at telling half truths. So, the key for us is to be able to discern the *source* of a statement to tell whether it is true.

In this chapter, we will recap the things we have learned so far into a format that will help us identify the consistency of Satan's strategy. This is important so we can see how and where Satan is making his attacks and to help us figure out how to resist these attacks. Once we see clearly what Satan is trying to do, we can have a new appreciation for the importance of developing a close relationship with God.

Contradictions to Christianity

Since this book is being written from a Christian viewpoint, let's take a look at some of the important beliefs of Christianity and how they are contradicted by other world religions, New Age prophets, or Satan himself. In addition to all these things, some people have just made up their own beliefs that have no factual support. I am not going to say that Satan is behind all of these contradictions; however, he would certainly agree with them because they are consistent with his agenda. Think about this - Satan's objective is to pull people away from God, specifically by discrediting Jesus. You will not see Satan arguing with any of the Eastern religions because they have already avoided God. You don't see Satan or his evil spirits making statements that contradict the teachings of Buddha, because Buddhism does not embrace God. There is a good reason that Satan is focused on Christianity, and it is that he *knows* that Jesus is the Son of God. One way in which Satan can keep people away from Christianity is to convince people that Jesus is not the only way to God.

We need to acknowledge that many world religions were founded prior to Christianity and that the beliefs of Christianity created many of the contradictions with existing world religions. But the Eastern religions had already ignored God before the birth of Jesus. Judaism is the only religion to have embraced God prior to the birth of Jesus, but Judaism has rejected Jesus as being the Son of God. The only major world-wide religion that was founded after Christianity is Islam, and that religion has also rejected Jesus as being the Son of God. Therefore, it would be fair to say that Islam created contradictions with Christianity, rather than vice versa.

The following section summarizes some of the major contradictions between Christianity and other religious beliefs and theories. In each section, I will show contradictory beliefs in italics, with the groups who support these beliefs in parentheses. Then, I will list the Christian beliefs along with the biblical references for these beliefs.

- *God is not a being, but rather an energy force that permeates the entire universe and exists in each of us. God is in everything, and everything is God (New Age). Mother Earth is a living being, a deity that should be worshiped (New Age).* God created the heavens and the earth, the land and seas and all living things. He is the Creator, not the creation! (Genesis 1:1-21)
- *We can become gods by achieving a higher level of consciousness (New Age, Hinduism). It is more important to focus on self awareness than whether there is a God (New Age, Buddhism).* There is only one God, the Creator of the universe, who is greater than any other gods that man invents. (Exodus 20:3)
- *Man is born sinless and stays that way unless he rebels against God (Islam). There is no such thing as sin. Sin is just failing to understand the point of human existence (New Age).* Because of Adam and Eve yielding to Satan, man is born with a sinful nature and needs to ask God for forgiveness. (Genesis 3:11-19, 2 Corinthians 5:21) *All* of us are considered sinners in God's eyes. (Romans 3:23)
- *Jesus was born of a human mother and either an ET or human father (New Age). Jesus is the son of Joseph (Judaism, Islam).* Jesus was born

to the Virgin Mary, who became pregnant by the Holy Spirit. (Matthew 1:19-20)

- *God did not have a son. Jesus was the son of Joseph and was a great prophet (Judaism, Islam). Jesus is not the Son of God (New Age).* Jesus was the Son of God, the Messiah promised by God to the Israelites. (Luke 1:26-35, Luke 8:28, John 20:31, Matthew 16:13-20)

- *Jesus is a human and could not have existed prior to the time he was born (Judaism, Islam).* Jesus was with God during the creation of the universe and is eternal just like God. (John 1:1, John 8:58, John 17:5, Matthew 28:20)

- *The miracles performed by Jesus either did not happen or were facilitated by aliens using their advanced technologies (New Age).* Jesus performed miracles while he was on Earth to demonstrate that the Spirit of God was within him. (Acts 2:22, John 10:24-26, John 10:31-33)

- *Many paths lead to God or whatever you call god (New Age, Buddhism, Hinduism, popular belief). There are multiple gods (Hinduism). Jesus was just a prophet and is not needed for access to God (Judaism, Islam).* Jesus says that he is the *only* way to God the Father. (John 14:6)

- *Truth is relative. Each person can define their own god. Each of us is truth because God is in us and we are gods (New Age).* Jesus says that he is the way, the truth, and the life. (John 14:6)

- *Jesus died but was not resurrected (Judaism). Jesus was not crucified; instead Judas was a substitute for Jesus on the cross (Islam).* Jesus, who was sinless, died for forgiveness of our sins. He rose on the third day and ascended into heaven. (Mark 16:6-7, Mark 15:37-39, 2 Corinthians 5:21)

- *Satan is not a real being but just a symbol of evil. Hell is not a real place but just a symbol for punishment by God (New Age, popular belief).* Satan is a fallen angel who was created by God. He is a being and is referred to as such many places in the Bible. (Ezekiel 28:12-17, 2 Corinthians 11:14-15, John 8:44) Hell is a place of torment where Satan, the other fallen angels, and those who reject

Jesus will spend eternity. (Matthew 5:29, Matthew 23:33, 2 Peter 2:4, Revelation 20:10)

- *Good works determine how we are judged (popular belief). We must obey God's rules and laws to gain favor with him (Judaism, Islam). We can obtain Nirvana and complete happiness by obtaining a higher level of consciousness (Buddhism, New Age).* We can obtain eternal life only by accepting Jesus as our Lord and Savior (salvation by faith instead of works). (Acts 16:31, John 3:16)

- *We don't need to believe. We just need to improve our consciousness to find God. Feeling is more important than believing (Buddhism, New Age). Jesus is a prophet rather than our Lord (Judaism, Islam).* If you *believe* that Jesus Christ is Lord, then you will be saved. (John 3:16)

- *Salvation occurs on Earth, and is a state of mind. Heaven is not an actual place (New Age, Buddhism). We do not go to heaven; instead we are reincarnated over and over until we achieve perfection on our own (New Age, Buddhism, and Hinduism).* Salvation occurs when our physical bodies die and our spirits live forever in heaven with God. This salvation is available only through Jesus. (John 14:2-3)

- *Reincarnation allows us to try to get better in another life. At some point, we can become like God by continuing to improve (New Age, Buddhism).* Man only physically dies one time and only has one chance to get right with God. We must get right with God during our lifetime. (Hebrews 9:27-28)

- *Those with archaic beliefs will be removed from the Earth at some point so that those who are more progressive can take the Earth to a higher level of consciousness (New Age).* Jesus will return to Earth during the end times, suddenly and without notice, to retrieve his followers and save them from some or all of the judgments to be poured out upon the earth. (1 Thessalonians 4:16-17) Jesus will return in the clouds in the same manner as when he was taken up to heaven after the resurrection. (Acts 1:9-11) Those who are left behind will experience the greatest tribulation since the world was created. (Matthew 24:21)

- *We need to support the coming great world leader and help to usher in the New World Order. This is a time of great rejoicing and revelation (New Age).* During the end times, an instrument of Satan called the Antichrist will appear. He will unify the world into a single world government and religion and destroy those who don't agree with him. He will be the personification of evil. There will be no rejoicing. (1 John 2:22, Revelation 13:1-8)

- *Those left behind after the rapture will usher in the New Age and move with Earth into the fourth dimension. Jesus will not return after the rapture (New Age). God will send a messiah to be an earthly king for the Jews, but this will not be Jesus (Judaism).* Jesus will return again to Earth in the end times to defeat the Antichrist and perform the final judgment on all who have rejected him (the second coming). Jesus is the Messiah that the Jews have been waiting on. Those who reject God will be condemned to spend eternity in hell. (Revelation Chapters 16, 17, 18, 19)

- *Heaven is just a state of mind and is not a place which is "up there" (New Age). You can get to heaven by being a good person (popular belief).* Heaven is a place where God and Jesus live and where *Christians* will be when they obtain their spiritual bodies. (John 6:38, John 14:1-3) The only way to get to heaven is through accepting Jesus as our Savior. (John 14:6)

What can we learn from this comparison of beliefs? The first thing is that some of the contradictions with Christianity are actually contradictions with each other! All of these different theories just can't be right. If a person is looking outside the Bible for answers, how could he possibly pick one of these alternate views, other than just picking the one that he wants to believe? There is no basis for establishing truth once we get away from what God says in the Bible.

Second, there seems to be a pattern here. Almost every significant event discussed or point made in the Bible has been contradicted by some group. The key principles in the Bible that were not in conflict with the early religions have been addressed more recently by the New Age groups, including their channelers, and by Islam. In fact, events that have not even happened yet such as the rapture and the second coming are already under attack by the New Age groups. I am convinced that Satan is influencing these attacks. The false prophets predicted in the Bible are already here. They are providing us with attractive, appealing concepts saying that we don't need Jesus because there are many other ways to God. They are telling us that heaven is for good people rather than those who have accepted Jesus. They are telling us what many *want* to hear instead of what they *need* to hear. This strategy reveals Satan's talent for finding our human weaknesses and appealing to them.

Another thing we can realize from this study is that no religion is under attack like Christianity. As we said earlier, this is where Satan's focus lies. You don't really see all the non-Christian religions arguing with each other. The New Age movement has embraced the Eastern Religions because they don't believe in the God Jehovah. If you read a lot of New Age literature and some of the channelers transcripts, there is a focus on denying the deity of Jesus. Since Judaism and Islam do not support the deity of Jesus, the New Age theories are a direct attack on Christianity. Christianity remains the only religion that supports the deity of Jesus, and therefore no other religions agree with this belief.

We also know that Satan is focused on Christianity based on the statistics we looked at earlier in this book. Christianity is suffering from attrition right now. Traditional churches are seeing their attendance growth level off or even decline. Many churches are changing their names to try to appeal to younger generations that don't want to associate with traditional denominations. We don't see these same trends in other religions to the extent that we are seeing them in Christianity. These trends point out the effectiveness of Satan's influence.

We need to think about why Satan is focused on destroying Christianity. Is it because Satan was in heaven at one time and knows that Jesus is the Son of God? Is it because Satan is not bound by our space-time dimension and he can see the future? Is it because Satan knows that Jesus is coming back, and Christians are the only group who will be rescued from the tribulation by Jesus? The answer to all of these questions is yes. Even Satan does not deny that the rapture will occur. Even Satan's demons know that Jesus is the Son of God, since they addressed him this way when they encountered him. Satan and his evil spirits know they are running out of time, and they are turning up the heat on Christians.

As a way to provide more clarity on how Satan has stepped up attacks on Christianity, let's remove other world religions from the comparison we just looked at and just focus on Satan's attacks that have occurred in the last fifty years. We can see Satan's position easily in just looking at these messages that have come from Satan or his evil spirits:

- God did not create the universe.
- Jesus is not the Son of God.
- Jesus' biological father was Joseph or another human.
- Mary was not a virgin.
- Jesus did not perform the miracles recorded in the Bible.
- Jesus was not crucified on the cross.
- Jesus was not resurrected from the dead.
- The rapture will remove people who don't fit in the New Age.
- The Antichrist is not evil but rather a great leader who will usher in the New Age.
- We can all become gods.

Satan's greatest deceptions of all are probably the deceptions related to himself. These are the deceptions that Satan does not really exist and there is no such thing as sin or hell. Can you imagine being such a good liar that you could convince someone that you don't exist?

You may be thinking that you have never had an encounter with Satan and don't feel that he has any influence on you. Perhaps you have adopted some alternate beliefs just because you thought they made sense. Perhaps you aren't the most dedicated Christian, but you think that you are still a pretty good person with good morals. If so, then please don't forget these things: Satan is an evil spirit who influences our minds. Satan can convince us that something that is completely wrong is acceptable. Satan can convince us that what we want is more important than what God wants. Satan can convince us that what we believe is correct even if it is the opposite of what is contained in the Bible. He makes these things attractive to us so we will feel good about ourselves. Have you stopped to consider how God feels about these deceptions? Have you ever asked God to help you understand the truth?

How can anyone justify believing in certain parts of Christianity and certain parts of other religions, especially when beliefs are completely contradictory to each other? If we believe that Jesus provides eternal life for us, then we need to believe *everything* he said. Trusting in Jesus means having a relationship with him and letting him help us eliminate sin from our lives. Without this relationship, we can only say that we know who Jesus is, rather than saying that we know him personally. Look at what Jesus says about casual believers:

> "Not everyone who says to me, 'Lord, Lord,' will enter the kingdom of heaven, but only he who does the will of my Father who is in heaven. Many will say to me on that day, 'Lord, Lord, did we not prophesy in your name, and in your name drive out demons and perform many miracles?' Then I will tell them plainly, 'I never knew you. Away from me, you evildoers!' Therefore everyone who hears these words of mine and puts them into practice is like a wise man who built his house on the rock. The rain came down, the streams rose, and the winds blew and beat against that house; yet it did not fall, because it had its foundation on the rock. But everyone who hears these words of mine and does not put them into practice is like a foolish man who built his house on sand. The rain came down, the streams rose, and the winds blew and beat against that house, and it fell with a great crash." [1]

In these verses, Jesus is saying that you can't just call him Lord and get into the kingdom of heaven. He is describing casual believers who just know who he is. The implication is that the casual believers know that he is the Son of God because they have been doing good works in the name of Jesus. When Jesus calls casual believers "evildoers," he means sinners. He is referring to people who know who he is but don't change their lifestyle and don't obey him. (As we saw earlier, about two thirds of U.S. adults fall into this category). He calls them fools for listening to his words and not putting them into practice. When Jesus was on Earth, he often criticized the Pharisees for behaving like fools. They were religious on the outside and very strict in enforcing their rules, but on the inside they were selfish people who were more concerned with their own importance than with bringing people closer to God. Sadly, our churches today have many people in them who don't have a personal relationship with Jesus. Even worse, many people are not attending church at all and have no interest in building a relationship with Jesus.

In the scripture that we just read, Jesus says that heaven is "only for he who does the will of my Father...". What is God's will for us? It is very simple:

- That we would believe in Jesus and accept him as our Savior (John 6:40).
- That we would love God with all our heart, soul, mind and strength (Mark 12:30).
- That we would love our neighbors as ourselves (Mark 12:31). This means to treat other people the way we want to be treated.

Did you notice all the verbs in the previous paragraph? God's will is that we would take action on these things and make him our focus.

Satan vs. Society

Earlier we talked about the decline in morality in our world. Are bad moral values caused by people moving away from God, or are bad moral values causing people to move away from God? I believe that it is some of each. A common objection to Christianity is that people don't want to change their lifestyle. The problem with this objection is that Christianity is not based on a set of rules and morals, contrary to a perception held by many people. In fact, God makes it clear that we are all sinners regardless of how we have behaved. Christianity provides us with a personal relationship with Jesus, which in turn makes us *want* to be more like him. If more people developed a relationship with Jesus, morality would automatically improve. The fact that many people have moved away from having this relationship has allowed Satan to get his foot in the door.

Satan's influence can be seen in many places in our modern society. He not only attacks Christian beliefs directly, but he is trying to remove God from our society. The United States was founded on principles of religious freedom. This means that we can worship however we choose without the government telling us what to do. However, this country was founded as "one nation, under God" and many official documents still contain references to God. Religious freedom means that we would not be persecuted if we wanted to adopt a religion other than Christianity. In countries where there is no religious freedom, the government tells everyone what to believe. In some countries, the head of the government is really a religious leader rather than an elected official. I am not aware of any cases in the history of the United States where the government told someone that they had to worship God because we were founded as one nation, under God.

The concept of separation of church and state is not in the United States Constitution! In spite of this, the U.S. Supreme Court uses this concept as a basis for interpreting law and validated it in one of their court cases. Our U.S. forefathers came here so they could worship God without any interference from the government. Somehow, the concept of separating church and state has been twisted into a different meaning. Today, it means that you can worship however you choose, but you must keep it to yourself. We can't discuss the Bible in school even though it is the world's greatest history book. We can't teach the biblical view of creation in many schools, but it is acceptable to teach evolution in spite of the lack of evidence for this theory. We can't post the Ten Commandments in a government building because it might imply that the government is endorsing the Bible. Praying in large groups is now considered to be an infringement on individual rights. The U.S. government, through a liberal Supreme Court, is now interfering with how we can worship God. Not only that, the Supreme Court has started legislating morality such as they did in legalizing abortion. America is governed "by the people and for the people," but have any of you been allowed to vote on any of these issues?

In the recent national election in the U.S., conservative Christians were labeled as haters, extremists, non-progressive, and many other things by the liberal politicians. Do they not realize (or care) that they are attaching these same labels to God? The Christians I know who are true believers think that our nation's morals should be based on God's definitions of morality as clearly defined in the Bible. The Bible makes it clear that God hates sin but not the sinner. The government certainly has the right to take something that God considers to be a sin and make it legal. But, making something legal doesn't make it right in God's eyes. We are clearly seeing a trend where the U.S. is moving away from Godly values. This trend reflects a failure to acknowledge that God is actually in charge of his creation and everything in it (Psalm 24:1).

I think there are more changes coming. Our pledge of allegiance still has the words "under God." Our currency contains the phrase "In God We Trust." Many government buildings also have this inscription. And, many of our official documents still refer to God. Many of our voting places are actually in churches. Surely Satan would love to eliminate these things from our society, and there are plenty of Americans lined up with him who will probably try to make it happen. If Satan doesn't get this done before the end times, then the Antichrist will surely take care of it.

In the Supreme Court case *Holy Trinity Church vs. U.S.* in 1892, the Supreme Court's unanimous opinion included a statement by Justice David Brewer that the United States is a Christian nation. Justice Brewer later acknowledged that this statement was not designed to set a legal precedent. However, it reflected the history and practices of the U.S. up until 1892. How did we get from being a Christian nation to one where the government wants to remove any mention of God? This change reflects the influence of Satan (who is using the doctrines of political correctness and tolerance to his advantage).

Our godless society is helping out Satan in other areas. Many stores quit selling Christmas trees a few years ago and started calling them

"Holiday trees." The commandment to not take the Lord's name in vain is generally ignored based on conversations that you might hear. Satan's influence on morals is obvious – he has convinced people that things considered sinful just fifty years ago are now considered acceptable. There is more, but this is enough to show the disturbing trends that are taking place.

If you study the Bible, you will see that the New World Order that will be implemented in the end times is actually a socialist government. Everyone wanting to buy or sell goods will be required to have a mark on their body indicating that the government has allowed them to do this. In the book of Revelation, this is called the "mark of the beast."

The way a socialist government functions is to get enough people dependent on the government so that the socialists are always re-elected. The government is designed this way to control the masses. The government may tell you if religion is allowed, and if so, what type. The Bible tells us that the Antichrist will try to eliminate Christianity during the end times and that Christians will be persecuted during this time. The socialist type of government fits right into Satan's plans. Based on the increasing number of entitlements in the U.S., it looks like we are moving in a socialist direction.

We may not be around for the end times. If not, our end times occurs when we die. We can prepare for our end times by studying the Bible, joining with a group of believers, and praying to God for his guidance and wisdom. Best of all, we don't need to resist Satan by ourselves. In fact, it is impossible for us to resist Satan without God's assistance. The Bible says that God will protect us: "Put on the full armor of God so that you can take your stand against the devil's schemes." [2] God will help us identify and recognize Satan's schemes and then give us the armor we need to resist them. Satan's lies and deceptions are occurring right now, and we need God to help us determine truth. The fact that only God can protect us from Satan tells us a lot about God's power and majesty.

Summary

In this chapter we learned about Satan's attacks against God and Christianity, and how they consist of lies and deceptions:

- Satan has contradicted or counterfeited most of the key points of the Bible including prophecies concerning the future.
- Satan's lies and deceptions will increase in the end times.
- Satan's lies and deceptions are designed to be attractive to us.
- Satan knows that Jesus is the Son of God, and therefore focuses his attacks on Christians.
- Satan's influence has changed America from a Christian nation to one where the government restricts Christianity.
- We cannot resist Satan without God's assistance.
- Jesus can provide us wisdom, protection from Satan, and salvation from sin, but only if we make the decision to accept him while we are still living.

CHAPTER 9:

Summary of the End Times

So far, we have seen that there is a spiritual war underway between the forces of good and evil and both sides want our allegiance. We have seen that the evil forces rely on attractive lies and deceptions, thus making it difficult for us to determine the truth and what to believe. Now we need to take a look at the future to get a complete picture of who God is and how his plan for us comes together. God's final judgment on humanity will take place in what is known as the end times. Most people are familiar with the term *Armageddon* and know that it has become a symbolic term for the end of our age or the end of the world as we know it. However, there are quite a few other events that will take place before the final battle of Armageddon occurs.

End times is the term I am using to denote the seven year period from the revealing of the Antichrist until the final return of Jesus. This term is also widely used to denote a much longer period of time (which we are currently in), but I am going to use the narrower definition for convenience. We don't know exactly when the seven year period will begin, but we can look at the signs given to us in the Bible and tell that we are getting close.

There seems to be quite a fascination with the end times based on the attention that has been given to movies about the end of the world and the attention given to false prophets who have declared specific dates when the world would end. Yet, in spite of this fascination, I know many Christians who have not studied the book of Revelation to understand God's plan for the future. This is a book filled with symbolism that is confusing to many people. In this chapter, I will give you a brief summary of what will happen during the end times. The Bible makes a lot more sense when you see how the information in Revelation relates to God's history with us on Earth.

Biblical scholars have differing opinions about some of the symbolism in Revelation and the timing of certain events, including the event known as the rapture. In spite of the differing interpretations, the overriding message is clear – God is in control and he has given full authority to his Son Jesus to execute his final judgment on humanity. It is *only* through Jesus that we can be saved from the consequences of our sins. This may be a politically incorrect or offensive statement to you, but the Bible is very clear on this point!

What Are the End Times?

Let's look at the key events, terminology, and time periods that are part of the end times. Most of this information comes from the books of Revelation, Daniel, Matthew, Mark, and Thessalonians in the Bible.

There is considerable debate among Christian theologians about when the rapture will occur. Many experts believe it will occur prior to the tribulation period while others believe it will occur at some point during the tribulation or possibly at the end (simultaneous with the second coming). The important point is that we don't really know. Jesus makes it clear that *only* God knows when this will occur. It is not the purpose of this book to speculate about when this will occur. However, it *is* a purpose of this book to inform you that it will be a surprise and that you need to be ready for it.

The Church Age

We are currently in a period called the church age, which began with the resurrection of Jesus almost two thousand years ago. This age represents the great growth period for Jesus' church. During this period, billions of people have accepted Jesus as their Savior. About one third of the world's population today calls themselves Christian.

False Prophets

Jesus tells us that there will be *many* false prophets prior to the reign of the Antichrist during the end times, and we are certainly seeing this prophecy come true. We have already seen that the Bible's definition of a false prophet is one who does not proclaim that Jesus is the Son of God. Also, anyone who decides that they can become a god is also a false prophet. Jesus warns us about false prophets: "Watch out that no one deceives you. For many will come in my name, claiming, 'I am the Christ,' and will deceive many." [1]

Birth Pangs

The Book of Matthew uses this term to describe the changes that will take place on Earth during the church age. These changes include increased wars, natural disasters, and famines. These disasters become more intense and more frequent as we get closer to the rapture. The definition of a birth pang is "a repetitive pain that occurs during childbirth." As the mother gets closer to the birth of a child, the pains become more intense and more frequent. Jesus describes these events as birth pangs to give us clues as to when the end times is near. It is fairly obvious that many of these disasters are already occurring and are increasing in intensity.

The Rapture

The rapture is the time when Jesus returns in the air to collect his followers and spare them from some or all of the tribulation. All Christians will be lifted up to meet Jesus in the sky. The supernatural nature of this event will make it clear that it was caused by God. Jesus tells us to be on the lookout at all times, because "No one knows about that day or hour, not even the angels in heaven, nor the Son, but only the Father." [2] Jesus made this comment when his disciples asked him about his second coming, but it applies to the rapture as well.

The Tribulation

The term *tribulation* is used by Bible scholars to refer to the period when God pours out his judgment on the inhabitants of the earth. Many scholars believe that the true tribulation period starts at the midpoint of the seven year end times period when the Antichrist sets himself up to be worshiped in the Jewish temple. Jesus describes the tribulation period as follows: "...there will be great distress, unequaled from the beginning of the world until now—and never to be equaled again." [3] It is hard to describe how bad this period of time will be. If we took all the natural disasters, plagues, wars, and diseases that we have seen so far and added them together, they would not equal the disasters that will occur during the tribulation.

It is significant to note that the nation of Israel was restored by the United Nations in 1948. Restoring Israel was one of the things required to happen before the tribulation period could begin. We also know from the Bible that the Jewish temple in Jerusalem will be rebuilt at some point prior to the tribulation period.

The Antichrist

The Bible describes the "spirit of the antichrist" as every spirit that does not acknowledge that Jesus is the Son of God (1 John 4:3). These spirits have been around since the first century A.D. The Bible tells us that the human Antichrist will begin as a peaceful leader but will turn to military force to accomplish his objectives. Satan will give power to the Antichrist and his False Prophet to perform miracles to deceive people. His reign will be one of terror for all people because the Antichrist will be filled with the evil spirit of Satan. He will be unable to do anything to counteract the power and majesty of God, but he will still demand that he be worshiped as God. He will force people to be his followers by demanding that they wear the "mark of the beast" to buy or sell any goods. The reign of the Antichrist will be the worst period to be alive in the history of the world.

At the end of the tribulation period, the Antichrist will gather together all the armies of the world to destroy Israel. The armies will gather at

Armageddon, where they will be defeated by Jesus and his angels as they return to Earth.

The Judgments

During the tribulation period, God will bring judgments upon the world's inhabitants that are unlike anything that has been seen before. God will allow the Antichrist to rule the world for a time during which the Antichrist will kill millions of people. During the Antichrist's reign, God will create a series of disasters including famine, plagues, earthquakes, disturbances in the heavens, destruction of the seas and fresh waters, fires, locusts, scorching sun, and darkness. Billions of people will die as a result of these disasters. Although these are clearly judgments against those who rejected him, the God-created events will be supernatural so that everyone will know that he is God. Even so, many people will to reject him up to the time of their death.

The Second Coming

The second coming of Jesus marks the end of the tribulation period. This event is called the second coming because the first coming of Jesus was around two thousand years ago. Jesus describes the second coming as follows:

> "Immediately after the distress of those days the sun will be darkened, and the moon will not give its light; the stars will fall from the sky, and the heavenly bodies will be shaken. At that time the sign of the Son of Man will appear in the sky, and all the nations of the earth will mourn. They will see the Son of Man [Jesus] coming on the clouds of the sky, with power and great glory. And he will send his angels with a loud trumpet call, and they will gather his elect from the four winds, from one end of the heavens to the other." [4]

Jesus comes back to rescue Israel because of Israel's cry for help from God. At this time, Jesus will gather his believers who survived the tribulation, and the bodies of the believers who were killed during the tribulation will be raised to live with Jesus during the millennium. The Antichrist and his False Prophet will be thrown into the lake of fire (hell). Then, Satan will be locked up in the earth so that he cannot torment the inhabitants of Earth for one thousand years.

The Millennium

Millennium is a term meaning one thousand years. This period is the time when Jesus Christ will reign on Earth with his followers including the restored nation of Israel. The people of Israel will realize that Jesus is the Messiah, and they will worship him. Jerusalem will be the center of his kingdom, and believers from throughout the world will come there to worship Jesus. During this time, Jesus will fulfill the unfulfilled prophecies in the Bible concerning the nation of Israel. The best term we can use to describe the millennium is utopia. The earth has not seen an environment like this since before Adam and Eve sinned in the Garden of Eden.

Final Judgment

At the end of the millennium, Satan will be released for a short time. He will be allowed to tempt the inhabitants of the world to get them to turn away from Jesus. Satan will gather a great army and surround Jerusalem to defeat Jesus, but fire will come down from heaven and destroy the army. Satan will then be thrown into the lake of fire forever. All of the unbelieving dead (i.e. those who are not Christians) are then raised and judged by Jesus. If anyone's name is not found in the Book of Life, they are thrown into the lake of fire for eternity. The Book of Life is simply a list of those who have accepted Jesus as their Savior and Lord. After the final judgment, Jesus will reign with his followers forever in a new heaven on Earth.

Are We In the End Times?

Do you believe we are in the end times already? There are certainly some things going on in the world that indicate we are getting close. As I started writing this section of the book, an earthquake that registered 8.9 on the Richter scale occurred near Japan, creating significant devastation and a Tsunami that reached as far as California. This earthquake was one thousand times stronger than the one that devastated Haiti in early 2010! A few weeks later we watched one of the worst tornado outbreaks in U.S. history occurring in the Southern and Midwestern portions of the U.S. This was followed by the deadly Joplin, Missouri tornado. On top of all the devastating weather, there is continued rebellion and fighting in the Middle East and terrorists trying to get their hands on nuclear and biological weapons.

The Bible tells us the signs of the end times that we need to watch for. If we see these events happening, and notice that they are increasing in intensity and frequency, then we will know that that we are getting close to the beginning of the end times period. Every day that goes by is one day less that you have to get right with God.

Jesus gives us the signs that will tell us when the end times is near:

> "When you hear of wars and revolutions, do not be frightened. These things must happen first, but the end will not come right away. Then he said to them: Nation will rise against nation, and kingdom against kingdom. There will be great earthquakes, famines and pestilences in various places, and fearful events and great signs from heaven." [5]

Let's look at some of these events individually.

Wars

The earth has experienced wars throughout its history. Our modern wars have clearly increased in scope and intensity. World War II was the deadliest ever, causing the death of approximately 50 million people, including civilians and around 6 million innocent Jews. People said that World War II would be the last great war, but since then we have seen the Korean War, Vietnam War, Desert Storm (Iraq), and the War on Terror (which may last for a while). These are just the wars involving the United States. There have also been major conflicts in several African nations, the Middle East, Europe and Asia, and deaths caused by governments oppressing their own citizens. Each war creates more tragedy and more loss of human life. We now possess technologies such as nuclear warheads, chemicals, and biological agents that could wipe out the entire planet if we used them.

It is unsettling to know that Iran is a nation currently experimenting with nuclear power and probably nuclear weapons. The President of Iran has already made inflammatory statements about the nation of Israel. In fact, Israel is surrounded by countries who are its enemies. There is so much unrest and hatred in the Middle East that it is easy to see that the great battles in the end times will take place in this area of the world, just as described in the book of Revelation.

Earthquakes

According to the U.S. Geological Survey, the annual number of earthquakes worldwide has stayed somewhat consistent since the year 2000. However, in looking at the breakdown by intensity, there was a large jump between 2006 and 2007 in large earthquakes (6.0 or higher). The years after 2004 all appear to be more active than the ten or twenty year averages prior to that time. In a normal year, there is one earthquake with an 8.0 or higher magnitude, but there were four in 2007. A 9.0 or higher earthquake occurs on average once every twenty years. The earthquake in Japan in early 2011 was officially rated at 9.0 on the Richter scale. The numbers support the theory that earthquakes are currently increasing in number and intensity. We also seem to be in a cyclical pattern when looking at totals back to around 1900. There was a peak in the 1940s, then a leveling off, and now an increase again. This is a pattern similar to birth pangs.

Famines

Are we seeing food and water shortages today? Absolutely! As far as fresh water, we are in the middle of a worsening crisis. Look at these statistics from the United Nations:

- By 2050, between 2 billion and 7 billion people will be faced with water scarcity.
- 1.2 billion people already lack access to safe drinking water.
- 2.4 billion people do not have access to proper sanitation facilities. This means raw sewage is being dumped into the earth and its fresh water lakes and rivers.
- In developing countries, 80 percent of illnesses are water related.
- Water usage is increasing at a faster rate than population growth.
- Increased water shortages will reduce agricultural production, creating food shortages and driving up prices. [6]

Not only do we have a water crisis, but the water crisis will actually make the food crisis worse. The vast majority of water consumption today is used for agricultural production. Water will become as precious as oil in the twenty first century.

What about the food crisis? Famine is now a bigger, more intense crisis than it has ever been. The United Nations has stepped up to provide part of the solution by helping out underdeveloped countries. Here is part of the U.N.'s assessment of the situation as of mid-2008:

> "The world food situation is rapidly being redefined. Unprecedented increases in the price of food and commodities is of major significance and represent a challenge of global proportions that has affected millions of people and particularly the most vulnerable, including the urban poor. It has also triggered violent protests in over 25 countries in Asia, Africa and Latin America and the Caribbean. Mounting hunger and severe malnutrition is increasingly evident. Until the current crisis, hunger had been slowly decreasing, but there were still about a billion undernourished people. Now their numbers are

growing. The welfare of billions of people has been threatened by the recent sharp increases in food prices, while at least three billion food-stressed people will bear the brunt of the crisis." [7]

Based on the U.N. assessment, about one-sixth of the earth's population does not have enough to eat. According to the humanitarian organization CARE, around six million children under the age of five die each year from hunger. Never before have this many people in the world suffered from hunger.

Pestilences

Pestilence is a synonym for a plague or epidemic. We don't have to look too far to find an epidemic that affects our society today. The AIDS epidemic is the largest worldwide health problem, outside of famine, that we are dealing with. It was very discouraging to recently see in the news that the epidemic in the Southern U.S. is actually worse than what the experts had previously thought. In spite of all the public education and warnings that have been issued, people are still not taking the proper steps to prevent the spread of this disease.

Here are a few statistics that show the size of this problem:

- More than 22 million people have died from AIDS.
- Over 42 million people are living with HIV/AIDS, and three fourths of these are in Africa.
- There are over 5 million new infections each year. Half of these are in young people between 15 and 24.
- There are 14 million AIDS orphans and the number is continuing to increase. [8]

This is a tragedy by any measure. Yet, since the time of Christ there have been plagues much worse that this one. The Black Plague, influenza, and smallpox have killed hundreds of millions of people. Today, we are still worried about influenza strains that adapt in new forms each year and could kill millions of people. Because of population growth and air travel today, these diseases can spread faster than ever and affect more people. Not only that, but terrorists with biological weapons could create massive disasters.

Fearful Events

Does an unprovoked terrorist attack against innocent U.S. citizens qualify as a fearful event? I would think so. Were you afraid to get on an airplane after the 9/11 events occurred in 2001? The answer is apparently yes, because the airline industry suffered huge drops in passenger volume after this attack occurred. The events of September 11, 2001 will change our world for a long time.

We talked about earthquakes, but what about hurricanes, tornadoes, and other natural disasters? Hurricane Katrina in 2005 was the costliest hurricane in U.S. history, and one of the strongest hurricanes ever recorded. We can expect future hurricanes to be as damaging as this one as we continue to expand large population centers along the U.S. coastlines. We are currently in a down cycle for hurricanes in the U.S. When this trend reverses, it will be one more sign that the birth pangs we were warned about are taking place.

Outside the U.S., a deadly typhoon hit Myanmar (Burma) in 2008. The latest estimates are that 140 thousand people were killed or are missing, and hundreds of thousands were left homeless. The tsunami in the Indian Ocean in 2004 killed almost 300 thousand people in the countries it affected, making it by far the largest tsunami ever recorded.

The deadliest tornado on record occurred in 1989, and the deadliest cyclone on record occurred in 1970. Both of these were in Bangladesh. The deadliest flood occurred in 1931, reportedly killing two to three million people in China. All of these dates are fairly recent, considering that the prophecies that predicted these disasters were written two thousand years ago.

Our economic conditions are also creating a crisis. The U.S. and other nations are continuing to exist only by borrowing money. At some point, there is more debt than what a country can afford. When this occurs, spending is slashed (often affecting human welfare) and taxes are raised. The citizens end up paying more and getting less. We should expect continued economic and political stress as we get closer to the end times. These things will happen as part of God's plan to allow the Antichrist to ascend to power.

Signs from Heaven

Earlier in this chapter, we looked at the signs from heaven that will occur at the second coming of Jesus, but what about the ones that will occur prior to the rapture? This is harder to figure out because the Bible doesn't give us any details about what they are. Luke's gospel contains the phrase "signs from heaven," but Matthew and Mark do not include this phrase in their gospels. It is possible that this phrase is referring to some events that take place during the tribulation, but we just don't know for sure.

Spreading the Gospel

Jesus tells us that his gospel will be preached throughout the world before the end comes: "And this gospel of the kingdom will be preached in the whole world as a testimony to all nations, and then the end will come." [9] Jesus had been talking about the destruction of the temple when the disciples asked him this question: "'Tell us,' they said, 'when will this happen, and what will be the sign of your coming and of the end of the age?'" [10] The question "when will this happen" refers to the destruction of the temple in 70 A.D., but the "end of the age" question clearly refers to something else. This is further obvious when we see in Matthew 24:15 that Jesus refers to an end times prophecy in the book of Daniel.

The bottom line is that every ethnic people group must hear the gospel message before Jesus returns. The gospel message is that Jesus is the Son of God, who died on the cross and rose from the dead on the third day. He gave his life so that we might be saved.

Obsession with Self

The apostle Paul gives us a pretty clear picture of the self absorption that people will demonstrate as we near the end times:

> "But mark this: There will be terrible times in the last days. People will be lovers of themselves, lovers of money, boastful, proud, abusive, disobedient to their parents, ungrateful, unholy, without love, unforgiving, slanderous, without self-control, brutal, not lovers of the good, treacherous, rash, conceited, lovers of pleasure rather than lovers of God— having a form of godliness but denying its power. Have nothing to do with them. They are the kind who worm their way into homes and gain control over weak-willed women, who are loaded down with sins and are swayed by all kinds of evil desires, always learning but never able to acknowledge the truth." [11]

Paul is referring to things that will happen in the last days, but we are seeing this type of behavior and attitude right now! We are living in the "I want it now" generation. People are willing to borrow thousands of dollars on their credit cards and second mortgages to satisfy their selfish desires. We have totally confused the concept of wants versus needs. People have not learned that money can't buy happiness but only temporary pleasure that makes them want more. Perhaps God will use the financial crisis that started in 2008 to help us all realize how quickly our material possessions can disappear and that we need to focus on more permanent matters.

What about the people who have a "form of godliness but deny its power"? Our society is full of these people. They attend church because it appears to be the right thing to do or because they think that good works will get them into heaven, but they have no relationship with God. They hear the Word of God, but assume that it doesn't apply to them. They continue to learn, but do not acknowledge the truth because their actions do not change. They reject portions of the truth because it is not what they want to hear. The actions of these people keep many others away from our churches today.

We see also in these verses that people who are loaded down with sins will "worm their way into homes and gain control over weak-willed women." In a further description of these evil people, Paul tells us the "impostors will go from bad to worse, deceiving and being deceived." [12] You might think you are not letting any of these people into your house, but when was the last time you turned on your television? Deceivers have already come into your house through your television!

False Beliefs

The Bible even says that new beliefs such as many that we are seeing today will be a sign of the end times. The apostle Paul gives us a pretty good description of some of our modern religious theories:

> "The Spirit clearly says that in later times some will abandon the faith and follow deceiving spirits and things taught by demons. Such teachings come through hypocritical liars, whose consciences have been seared as with a hot iron. For the time will come when men will not put up with sound doctrine. Instead, to suit their own desires, they will gather around them a great number of teachers to say what their itching ears want to hear. They will turn their ears away from the truth and turn aside to myths." [13]

We have already seen the statistics that show that people are moving away from God. Paul predicted this almost two thousand years ago. How did he know that this would happen? How did he know that people would surround themselves with teachers who tell them what they want to hear? Only God could have provided this wisdom to him. The fact that this prophecy has come true tells us that we are nearing the end times. Have any of your own beliefs been influenced by your desire to just believe what you want to believe?

Jesus' Warnings

We have already seen that Jesus provides us with the signs to tell us that the end is near, and that he warns us about all the false prophets and how we should not be deceived by them. Jesus also warns us about the second coming, relating it to events during the time of Noah:

> "As it was in the days of Noah, so it will be at the coming of the Son of Man. For in the days before the flood, people were eating and drinking, marrying and giving in marriage, up to the day Noah entered the ark; and they knew nothing about what would happen until the flood came and took them all away. That is how it will be at the coming of the Son of Man [Jesus]. Two men will be in the field; one will be taken and the other left. Two women will be grinding with a hand mill; one will be taken and the other left." [14]

What is Jesus telling us here? He is telling us to not worry about when this event will happen but to focus on making sure we are ready at all times. In spite of all the signs and warnings that the Bible gives us, most of the world will just continue to be focused on day to day living and the pursuit of wealth and happiness. People will not be prepared because they have not taken time to build a relationship with God. Noah was prepared because he was faithful to God, and God warned him about the flood. Noah was saved from the flood because he obeyed God! Sadly, many people today want to do things their own way, rather than God's way. Don't "miss the boat" by putting off the decision to accept Jesus as your personal Savior while you are still living.

Another interesting analogy about the time of Noah was that there was so much sin that God finally got sick of it and basically wiped out the inhabitants of Earth. Even a group of angels had left heaven prior to the flood and sinned against God. So many people had turned away from God that God found Noah and his family to be the only ones worth saving. This analogy is appropriate for the end times, especially after the Antichrist begins his reign in Jerusalem. Many will turn away from God both before and during this period.

The comparison to the time of Noah also provides us with similarities for the second coming of Jesus. We learned earlier that there were four groups of people and spirits in the time of Noah:

- One (Enoch) who was evacuated prior to the destruction.
- Those who were faithful to God and were saved.
- Those who were not faithful to God and perished.
- Those who were locked up in the earth to wait on final judgment at a later date.

When the rapture occurs, Jesus will evacuate his faithful believers from the earth and spare them from some or all of the destruction. When Jesus comes back at the end of the tribulation, those who were faithful to him during the tribulation will be saved. Those who were not faithful to God will be cast into hell. Satan will be locked up in the earth for a thousand years to wait on his final judgment day. God's behavior during the time of Noah adds validity to his statements that he will cause the events described in Revelation to happen.

Do You Believe?

How much of what we have covered in this book so far do you believe? Is there something in your past or in your knowledge box that keeps you from accepting God's Word as being true? The end times is a difficult area to study. Many of the things that are revealed to us are just not logical. For example, how could millions or billions of humans be levitated up into the sky during the rapture? Why would God throw people into the lake of fire just because they don't believe in Jesus? Why is the Antichrist considered to be evil when the New Age belief is that a great new leader is coming to unify the world and create lasting peace?

These answers are all in the Bible. I have quoted a very small percentage of the Bible so far in this book. The verses we have looked at show us that God is in control. There is nothing we can do to change his plan and how he intends to execute it. Have you seen anything yet that might cause you to change your current beliefs about God? Have you seen anything that indicates that God has changed over time and he needs to be redefined by our modern society?

Skeptics may say that all of the signs Jesus told us to watch for are our own fault. For example, we have not taken care of the Earth. Our pollution and waste have created global warming, which in turn is increasing natural disasters. We have been poor stewards of the riches that God gave us. However, Jesus made these statements almost two thousand years ago. How did he know this was going to happen? He knows because he is the Son of God, and he sees the future. Also, these events are happening because they are part of God's plan.

The Bible tells us that many will become doubters because the end times has been prophesied for two thousand years and it still has not occurred. The apostle Peter says:

> "First of all, you must understand that in the last days scoffers will come, scoffing and following their own evil desires. They will say, 'Where is this 'coming' he promised? Ever since our fathers died, everything goes on as it has since the beginning of creation.' But they deliberately forget that long ago by God's word the heavens existed and the earth was formed out of water and by water. By these waters also the world of that time was deluged and destroyed." [15]

People will conveniently forget that God already destroyed the world by water. God will keep his promise and destroy the world by fire in the end times. People will scoff at those who believe that Jesus is coming back, but Jesus will keep his word and will return based on God's timing.

We need to be careful because the increase in disasters and wars prior to the rapture could cause us to focus more attention on ourselves rather than God. We need to realize that these are events that must happen as part of his plan. So far, God has been implementing his plan exactly as described in the Bible. Is there any reason to doubt that God will continue to do this in the future?

Where in any of the verses in Revelation or other parts of the Bible does it say that there are multiple ways to God? Where does it say that you can get to heaven by being a good person? It is fairly obvious that the events in Revelation revolve around the return of Jesus and his defeat of Satan. The only people who will be saved before or during the tribulation are the ones who accept Jesus as their Savior. If we fail to accept Jesus, then we will be thrown into the lake of fire. We cannot blame God if this happens – the result totally depends on our actions.

If you have some religious beliefs that conflict with the Bible, where did they come from? Are they beliefs that you figured out on your own or learned by watching television? Wouldn't God have inspired other books containing this information if he needed to? The truth is that there is only one way to God, and this will be proven in the end times.

As a Christian, I have a personal relationship with Jesus that I would not want to change. Why would I consider exploring some other religion to find a different way to God? The only reason I would do this would be if I did *not* have a personal relationship with Jesus. Perhaps the reason that so many people believe that there are alternate ways to God is because they have not experienced the true benefits of having a personal relationship with Jesus. Once you have this relationship, there is no reason to look anywhere else for God.

Summary

The end times represents the time period where Jesus executes God's final judgment on the world. Here is a recap of what we have covered in this chapter:

- The rapture of Christians will take place at some point prior to or during the tribulation. Christians, both dead and alive, will be taken up in the air to spend eternity with Jesus.
- The signs that Jesus told us to watch for indicate that we are getting close to the end times.

- We need to be ready for the rapture to happen at any moment because Jesus warns us that it will occur without warning.
- The tribulation will be the worst period in the history of humanity. Billions will be killed and persecuted during this period.
- Those who claim to know the date when the end times will begin are false prophets.
- There will be an increase in those who do not accept the truth of God before the end times begins. People will surround themselves with teachers who tell them what they want to hear.
- There will be an increase in the number of people who are self-absorbed and not willing to acknowledge God before the end times begins.
- At the end of the tribulation period, Jesus will return to Earth to defeat the Antichrist and his armies.
- Those who did not accept Jesus as their Savior will be thrown into the lake of fire when the final judgment occurs.

CHAPTER 10:

Significance of the End Times

You can see that the end times events we just reviewed are the final events in the spiritual war between good and evil. Only those who have accepted Jesus as their Savior will avoid the final, permanent casualty: eternity in hell. The end times events will occur because they are part of God's plan. While many of the events will be physical, the overall purpose is spiritual.

In this chapter we will look at the role of the key players in this final period of history. I think you will find their behavior to be consistent with what we have learned about them already.

Satan in the End Times

We have seen what Satan has done in the past, so let's look at what he might do in the future. First of all, we can assume that Satan will continue to lie and deceive people because that is his basic nature. He will accuse us before God, entice us into sin, and try everything he can think of to pull us away from Christianity.

Second, we can expect Satan to come up with some new tricks. We know this because the Bible spells them out for us. As we look at these, we will see that one of Satan's tricks is counterfeiting. This means that he will take an event that God caused to happen and will produce a copy of it to deceive us into believing that he is just as powerful as God. Here are some of the counterfeit events that we can expect to see in the future:

- <u>Performing signs and wonders (miracles)</u>. We saw Satan do this way back in the time of Moses. When God turned Moses' staff into a snake, the Egyptian sorcerers did the same thing. However, Moses' staff then swallowed up the Egyptian staffs, proving that the God of Moses was more powerful than the gods of Egypt (Exodus 7:8-13). In the end times, God will allow Satan to perform miracles through the Antichrist and the False Prophet. This will be a test for believers to see if they will remain true to God. Let's look at the verses that give us the details:

> "Then I saw another beast [the "False Prophet"], coming out of the earth. He had two horns like a lamb, but he spoke like a dragon. He exercised all the authority of the first beast [the Antichrist] on his behalf, and made the earth and its inhabitants worship the first beast, whose fatal wound had been healed. And he performed great and miraculous signs, even causing fire to come down from heaven to earth in full view of men. Because of the signs he was given power to do on behalf of the first beast, he deceived the inhabitants of the earth. He ordered them to set up an image in honor of the beast who was wounded by the sword and yet lived. He was given power to give breath to the image of the first beast, so that it could speak and cause all who refused to worship the image to be killed. He also forced everyone, small and great, rich and poor, free and slave, to receive a mark on his right hand or on his forehead, so that no one could buy or sell unless he had the mark, which is the name of the beast or the number of his name." [1]

This is pretty amazing stuff. The False Prophet will be able to perform miracles, even bringing fire down from heaven. He will deceive the inhabitants of Earth (just like Satan does). He even makes an image of the Antichrist that can speak and causes those who refuse to worship the Antichrist to be killed. Many people will be deceived by the powers that Satan grants to the False Prophet.

God's penalty for worshiping the Antichrist is pretty severe:

> 'If anyone worships the beast and his image and receives his mark on the forehead or on the hand, he, too, will drink of the wine of God's fury, which has been poured full strength into the cup of his wrath. He will be tormented with burning sulfur in the presence of the holy angels and of the Lamb. And the smoke of their torment rises for ever and ever. There is no rest day or night for those who worship the beast and his image, or for anyone who receives the mark of his name." This calls for patient endurance on the part of the saints who obey God's commandments and remain faithful to Jesus." [2]

The scriptures we just read make it clear that everyone will be require to choose between the Antichrist and Jesus during the end times. Anyone who chooses Jesus will not be allowed to buy or sell goods and services. Anyone who chooses the Antichrist will be allowed to buy or sell goods and services but will spend eternity in hell. Have you thought about what you would do in this situation? Would you remain loyal to Jesus if it meant that you would not be able to feed your family? When you have difficult decisions to make today, do you rely on God or rely on your own abilities? Please remember that ignoring Jesus is the same as rejecting him.

A common New Age belief is that the New World leader will provide worldwide peace. The Bible says that following the New World leader will lead people down the path to hell. Perhaps you don't believe in hell as a physical place, but this passage makes it clear that there is no rest day or night for those who worship the Antichrist, and that this torment is eternal. That sounds like hell to me!

- <u>Raising someone from the dead</u>. This of course is a total counterfeit of Jesus' resurrection. The book of Revelation describes this evil resurrection:

> "The dragon [Satan] gave the beast [Antichrist] his power and his throne and great authority. One of the heads of the beast seemed to have had a fatal wound, but the fatal wound had been healed. The whole world was astonished and followed the beast. Men worshiped the dragon because he had given authority to the beast, and they also worshiped the beast and asked, 'Who is like the beast? Who can make war against him?'" [3]

In the book of Revelation, the dragon refers to Satan and the beast is the Antichrist. We see here that the Antichrist is given Satan's power and great authority. In the end times, there will be so much evil that people will actually worship Satan and the Antichrist (not just because they have to in order to survive, but because they will want to). In particular, this passage tells us that the Antichrist will have a *fatal* wound, but this wound will be healed, and he will rise from the dead. This deception will likely cause many to believe that the Antichrist is a deity. This resurrection is orchestrated by Satan to fool people into thinking that he is just as powerful as God.

We see later in Revelation that God is allowing the Antichrist to rule for three and one half years. He also is allowing the Antichrist to slay the saints (Christians) who have decided to accept Jesus after the rapture:

> "The beast was given a mouth to utter proud words and blasphemies and to exercise his authority for forty-two months. He opened his mouth to blaspheme God, and to slander his name and his dwelling place and those who live in heaven. He was given power to make war against the saints

and to conquer them. And he was given authority over every tribe, people, language and nation. All inhabitants of the earth will worship the beast— all whose names have not been written in the Book of Life belonging to the Lamb that was slain from the creation of the world." [4]

God is allowing Satan to do these things because it is part of his plan for final redemption and judgment of the world.

If we look at all of this information together, we will see that Satan is actually going to develop a counterfeit trinity. Satan's trinity consist of himself (a counterfeit God), the Antichrist (a counterfeit Jesus who rises from the dead), and the False Prophet (a counterfeit Holy Spirit).

The Bible tells us that the Antichrist will be more than just a world leader: "He will oppose and will exalt himself over everything that is called God or is worshiped, so that he sets himself up in God's temple, proclaiming himself to be God." [5] Not only will he claim to be God, he will set himself up to be worshiped in the Jewish temple in Jerusalem. In Daniel 9, we see that the Antichrist will confirm a covenant with the Jews, only to turn on them later. The Bible says that he will break this treaty and take over the temple for his own use.

Many people will be fooled by these counterfeit acts, miracles, and signs to be performed by these instruments of Satan and will not be able to resist the demands of the Antichrist in the end times. Perhaps you are thinking that the end times will not begin during your lifetime, so you don't need to worry about it. However, we are already living in a time where people are being fooled by false prophets, lies, and false religious beliefs. The only chance we have to get right with God is while we are still living. I feel sorry for people who put this off too long and then never get a chance to accept Jesus.

Jesus confirms that we need to get right with God while we are living by telling this story:

"There was a rich man who was dressed in purple and fine linen and lived in luxury every day. At his gate was laid a beggar named Lazarus, covered with sores and longing to eat what fell from the rich man's table. Even the dogs came and licked his sores. The time came when the beggar died and the angels carried him to Abraham's side. The rich man also died and was buried. In hell, where he was in torment, he looked up and saw Abraham far away, with Lazarus by his side. So he called to him, 'Father Abraham, have pity on me and send Lazarus to dip the tip of his finger in water and cool my tongue, because I am in agony in this fire.' But Abraham replied, 'Son, remember that in your lifetime you received your good things, while Lazarus received bad things, but now he is comforted here and you are in agony. And besides all this, between us and you a great chasm has been fixed, so that those who want to go from here to you cannot, nor can anyone cross over from there to us.' He answered, 'Then I beg you, father, send Lazarus to my father's house, for I have five brothers. Let him warn them, so that they will not also come to this place of torment.' Abraham replied, 'They have Moses and the prophets; let them listen to them.' 'No, father Abraham,' he said, 'but if someone from the dead goes to them, they will repent.' He said to him, 'If they do not listen to Moses and the prophets, they will not be convinced even if someone rises from the dead.'" [6]

The Antichrist

The Antichrist is the central figure on Earth during the tribulation period. As we have already discussed, he will be an instrument of Satan. His mission is the same as Satan's – to rule the world and destroy God's people. We need to spend some time looking at the Antichrist to avoid being deceived and to appreciate God's role in our future. Much of our understanding about these future events will have application to our daily lives.

In the Bible, the book of Daniel implies that the Antichrist will rise to power and will convince several ruling powers of the world to side with him, initially through persuasion and eventually through force. It won't bother the Antichrist to kill as many innocent people as he needs to in order to achieve his objectives.

So, who is the Antichrist? The apostle Paul calls him the "man of lawlessness". [7] The Antichrist is called the "man of sin" in some Bible translations. He is clearly a man who is filled with the spirit of Satan. He will oppose everything related to God and will proclaim himself to be God. He will not implement the New World Order agenda of peace and harmony, but rather Satan's agenda.

How will we recognize the Antichrist? Paul says:

> "For the secret power of lawlessness is already at work; but the one who now holds it back will continue to do so till he is taken out of the way. And then the lawless one will be revealed, whom the Lord Jesus will overthrow with the breath of his mouth and destroy by the splendor of his coming. The coming of the lawless one will be in accordance with the work of Satan displayed in all kinds of counterfeit miracles, signs and wonders, and in every sort of evil that deceives those who are perishing. They perish because they refused to love the truth and so be saved." [8]

These verses tell us that Satan is already at work to implement his plan, but he is currently being restrained. These constraints will be removed by God at the appropriate time so that the Antichrist can begin his reign. At this point, only God knows who the Antichrist is and where he will come from.

Because the Antichrist is empowered by Satan, he will be a liar and deceiver just like Satan. He will be able to perform supernatural miracles, signs, and wonders because he will be granted Satan's powers. Many will be deceived by him because of their false religious beliefs that cause them to reject Jesus. Many of these false religious beliefs are already present in the world today.

The Bible does not contain a physical description of the Antichrist. What we know is that he will be convincing, a world political leader able to sway people to his way of thinking (by lies and deceit). Don't underestimate the power of slick-talking politicians! We have elected plenty of them in the United States.

We should not waste our time looking for the Antichrist based on what we think he will look or sound like. We will know him by his works! Therefore, we should watch for the spirit of the Antichrist, because this is the spirit of Satan. We know that the spirit of Satan inspires people to deny God and to deny that Jesus is the Son of God. The spirit of the Antichrist is already at work in our modern world. Instead of looking for the Antichrist, we should be looking for Jesus! Only Jesus can deliver us from our sins and an eternity in hell.

The book of Daniel describes one of the Antichrist's initial deeds: "He will confirm a covenant with many for one 'seven.' In the middle of the 'seven' he will put an end to sacrifice and offering. And on a wing of the temple he will set up an abomination that causes desolation, until the end that is decreed is poured out on him." [9] The first part of these verses tell us that the Antichrist will broker a deal with Israel and many other countries. The term *confirm a covenant* is actually a very strong phrase. In the original Greek, the word for confirm actually means to prevail from a position of strength. This could imply that the Antichrist is dealing with Israel from a position so strong that Israel really has no choice but to agree to this covenant. The term *seven* means a seven year period. So, the Antichrist's covenant will be for seven years, but in the middle of the seven year period, he will put an end to the Jewish sacrifices and offerings in the newly rebuilt Jerusalem temple. Then, he will set himself up as God in a wing of the temple and demand that he be worshiped. This is the abomination referred to in these verses. Instead of God being present in his holy temple, it will be Satan's puppet who demands that he be worshiped. This will be the point in time that the Jews realize that they have made a pact with the devil.

Jesus confirms that Daniel's prophecy is true: "So when you see standing in the holy place 'the abomination that causes desolation' spoken of through the prophet Daniel—let the reader understand— then let those who are in Judea flee to the mountains." [10] Jesus is warning the Jews to flee to a place that God will provide for them as soon as they see the Antichrist demand to be worshiped. The Antichrist will intensely persecute the Jews from this time forward.

The book of Revelation tells us that Satan will declare war on the Jews and the followers of Jesus: "When the dragon [Satan] saw that he had been hurled to the earth, he pursued the woman [Israel] who had given birth to the male child [Jesus]. The woman was given the two wings of a great eagle, so that she might fly to the place prepared for her in the desert, where she would be taken care of for a time, times and half a time, out of the serpent's reach. Then the dragon was enraged at the woman and went off to make war against the rest of her offspring—those who obey God's commandments and hold to the testimony of Jesus." [11] This means that halfway through the end times period, the Antichrist will begin to aggressively pursue the Jews and persecute Christians. However, the Jews will be out of his reach, so he will focus his attention on Christians. A "time, times and half" means three and one half years. During this time, *anyone* not worshiping the Antichrist will be killed.

The Antichrist will implement Satan's version of the New World Order. He will reward those who are loyal to him with positions of power and wealth (Daniel 11:39). He will try to remove all religions from the earth other than the one based on himself. He will destroy any countries and people who do not go along with him. (Note: the Iranian Parliament passed a law in September, 2008 requiring a mandatory death penalty for anyone who leaves the Muslim religion for another religion. This is the type of law we can expect when there is no separation of church and state, as in the New World Order). The main goal of the New World Order is a socialist worldwide government with a single worldwide religion. The objective is worldwide peace, but this objective can only be achieved by killing anyone who does not support the new agenda. The New World Order is a the path to destruction. Jesus warns us: "For wide is the gate and broad is the road that leads to destruction, and many enter through it." [12]

Islam in the End Times

We know that Muslims will play a major role in the end times for two simple reasons. First, they account for almost 25 percent of the world's population today and this percentage is growing. Second, there are huge numbers of Muslims living near the nation of Israel, which will be a focal point for many of the end times events.

Looking at population trends also points to the increased influence of Muslims in areas other than the Middle East. Muslims are becoming an increasing percentage of the population in Europe, and some estimates are that they could actually become a majority of the European population in this century. When this occurs, Muslims will occupy important positions in the government and have a major influence on how these countries are run. This trend is significant because many biblical scholars believe that the Antichrist will come from a united Europe – sort of a resurrected Roman Empire.

We are all familiar with the bombings and terrorist acts that have been performed by militant Muslims, but Muslims are spreading by simply moving to other countries, becoming part of society, and expanding their families. This same trend is happening in the United States. There were around one million Muslims in the U.S. in 2000. In 2012, the Muslim population in the U.S. was around two million.

As I mentioned earlier in this book, Shiite Muslims (also known as Shia) and some of the factions within Islam believe in the coming of a messiah they call the Mahdi. The Shiite Muslims represent a minority of Islam, with the Sunni group being the largest group of Muslims. However, Shiites are the majority group in Iran and Iraq, which may have implications for the end times.

Some of the beliefs about the end times that can be found in the Islamic religion are listed below (summarized from public domain web sites):

- The Mahdi will be fully human – a descendant of Muhammad.
- Before the coming of the Mahdi, there will be red death (sword) and white death (plague).

- The Mahdi will have a reign on Earth of at least seven years before the final judgment day.
- The Mahdi will come to Earth with Jesus, who will assist him in ridding the world of evil.
- The appearance of the Mahdi will also be accompanied by the appearance of Dajjal (the Antichrist).
- The Mahdi will win an apocalyptic battle with the Antichrist.
- The Arabs will take possession of their lands by throwing out the foreigners. This is probably a reference to the land of Israel.
- Fire will appear in the sky over Bagdad, Iraq (in the area formerly known as Babylon).

Obviously, there are some parallels between these beliefs and the end times documentation in the book of Revelation, but there are also significant differences. (We need to remember that the Bible was written several hundred years before the Qur'an.) The most important difference is that Muslims view Jesus as just a prophet rather than as the Son of God. I believe that the Bible contains God's revelations about the end times, and that there is no need to try to add anything to the scenarios he has given us.

The reason that the Mahdi beliefs are important is that they have been adopted by President Ahmadinejad of Iran. Iran is a wealthy nation that has been flexing its muscle after the election of President Ahmadinejad. In some well-publicized speeches, he has advocated the removal of Israel from their homeland and even made a statement that the Holocaust did not really happen. More importantly, many people believe that Iran is developing a nuclear weapons program and would not hesitate to use these weapons against Israel. Mr. Ahmadinejad has prayed in public several times for Allah to hasten the return of the Mahdi.

According to a recent article on CBNNews.com, President Ahmadinejad believes that a certain amount of chaos must be created before the Mahdi can appear, and he may believe that it is part of his divine mission to create this chaos. We have already seen that radical Islamic groups are attacking Christians and Jews in the name of Allah. Jesus warned us about this in

John 16:2: "… a time is coming when anyone who kills you will think he is offering a service to God." As you read this, how can you deny that Jesus knows what he is talking about? Is it possible that these radical groups will accelerate the beginning of the end times? Will this evolve into the ultimate "holy war" that radical Muslims have declared? Only God knows how all of this will play out.

Could Islam become the single worldwide religion that the Antichrist will implement during the first half of the end times period? Certainly it is possible, but we don't really know. Here are some things that might support this happening:

- Islam was spread by the sword initially, and the worldwide religion will be spread in a similar manner.
- The Antichrist could be a Muslim if current trends in Europe continue.
- When Christians are removed from the Earth during the rapture, Islam will become the world's largest religion.
- The worldwide religion will deny the deity of Jesus, which Muslims already deny.
- In the end times, people who refuse to adopt the worldwide religion will be beheaded, a practice that has been seen in some Muslim countries.
- According to the book of Revelation, the headquarters of the Antichrist's empire will be in Babylon, an ancient city in Muslim dominated Iraq.

These are interesting speculations that are not supported by the Bible. I am not saying that these things will occur because I am not a prophet and I don't want to contradict God's Word. In fact, God warns us in Revelation 22:18 to not add anything to, or take anything away from, the prophecies in the book of Revelation. What is clear from the Bible is that the Antichrist will be an enemy of Christianity and Judaism. Islam did not exist when the Bible was written, so there is no mention of it.

Jesus in the End Times

Jesus' role in the end times can be summarized as follows:

- He will appear either before or during the tribulation to remove his followers from the earth.
- He will appear at the end of the tribulation to defeat the Antichrist and his evil forces in the battle of Armageddon and bring God's punishment on the Antichrist and False Prophet.
- Jesus will live on Earth with his followers during the millennium.
- He will defeat Satan permanently in a final battle before casting him into hell.
- He will bring God's judgment against those who have rejected him.

Let's look at these events individually.

The Rapture

This great event is described in a passage that we looked at previously. "Those who are alive at this time will be caught up in the clouds to meet the Lord in the air." [13]

The word "Lord" in this passage is referring to Jesus. Jesus is consistently described using this term throughout the New Testament section of the Bible. The reason that Jesus is gathering his followers is to spare those who have trusted in him from some or all of the tribulation. We know that the Jews are God's chosen people, but they are not being taken in the rapture unless they have accepted Jesus.

Battle of Armageddon

Jesus' return for the battle of Armageddon is described in these verses:

> "Then I saw the beast [Antichrist] and the kings of the earth and their armies gathered together to make war against the rider on the horse [Jesus] and his army. But the beast was captured, and with him the false prophet who had performed the miraculous signs on his behalf. With these signs he had

deluded those who had received the mark of the beast and worshiped his image. The two of them were thrown alive into the fiery lake of burning sulfur. The rest of them were killed with the sword that came out of the mouth of the rider on the horse, and all the birds gorged themselves on their flesh." [14]

It is likely that the battle of Armageddon will be seen by the aggressors as a battle to destroy Israel, and they will not realize that their true foe is Jesus! We know that the rider on the horse is Jesus because of Revelation 19:16: "On his robe and on his thigh he has this name written: King of Kings and Lord of Lords." This is a clear reference to Jesus, who has been given this authority by God the Father. The description of the battle of Armageddon makes it clear that the power of Jesus exceeds greatly the power of Satan and his representatives. Those who are killed are those who were deceived by the Antichrist and the False Prophet.

The Millennium

The millennium is described in Revelation 20. An angel binds Satan in the Abyss for a thousand years. Those Christians who were beheaded because they refused to worship the Antichrist or his image will come to life and reign with Jesus on Earth for a thousand years. [15]

The millennium begins after the battle of Armageddon. Many theologians believe that the armies of heaven who come with Jesus to the battle of Armageddon will actually be Christians who have died prior to this event. There will be other Christians living on the Earth who became Christians during the tribulation. Those Christians who were martyred during the tribulation during this time will be raised. The rest of the dead do not come to life during this period – instead they will receive judgment at the end of the millennium. The key point of the millennium is that Jesus will reign on Earth. Satan will be locked up during this period.

A good question is "what happens to the Jews during this period"? We see that those who have rejected Jesus will be killed during the battle of Armageddon, as well as others who died during the tribulation. Since the Jews are God's chosen people, what will be their fate? From a logical standpoint, perhaps many Jews will accept Jesus when they see he is the one who has come back to defeat their enemies. But there is also biblical support that God will not abandon the Jews:

> "I do not want you to be ignorant of this mystery, brothers and sisters, so that you may not be conceited: Israel has experienced a hardening in part until the full number of the Gentiles has come in, and in this way all Israel will be saved. As it is written: 'The deliverer will come from Zion; he will turn godlessness away from Jacob. And this is my covenant with them when I take away their sins.' As far as the gospel is concerned, they are enemies for your sake; but as far as election is concerned, they are loved on account of the patriarchs, for God's gifts and his call are irrevocable. Just as you who were at one time disobedient to God have now received mercy as a result of their disobedience, so they too have now become disobedient in order that they too may now receive mercy as a result of God's mercy to you. For God has bound everyone over to disobedience so that he may have mercy on them all." [16]

This passage was addressed to Christians warning them not to be conceited because they had received God's grace (Jesus) and the Jews had not. God blinded the eyes of the Jews for a time so that they could not see or appreciate that Jesus was actually the Messiah. However, God's love for the Jews has not changed, and these verses show us that "all Israel will be saved". Does this mean that every Jew will become a Christian during the end times? It is not automatic - they must individually choose whether to accept Jesus. While their eyes are blinded by God, it will be understandable if they don't accept Jesus. But, God says that he will remove this restriction when "the full number of the Gentiles has come in". When would this be? Perhaps this will be near the end of the tribulation. People will have the opportunity to accept Jesus until the final battle of Armageddon (as long as they have not taken the mark of the beast) because God does not wish for anyone to perish.

The verses that we just looked at tell us that God has bound all of us to disobedience so that he can have mercy on us. This explains why he has allowed Satan to influence us and to have additional powers during the end times. God has given us Jesus as our Savior to demonstrate his mercy and grace. There is nothing we can do to earn or deserve this gift. It is available to anyone who wants to repent and accept Jesus. However, Revelation 14:9-10 tells us that there is no repentance available for those who take the mark of the beast.

Satan's final defeat

At the end of the millennium, Satan will be set loose for a time and allowed to deceive people. Many theologians believe this is so everyone living on the earth will have a final opportunity to choose Satan or Jesus. Satan will lead many astray but will be defeated permanently by Jesus. The Bible tells us that Satan will deceive many people when he is released, gather nations around the great city for battle against Jesus, and that the rebels will be destroyed by fire from heaven. Satan will then be confined to hell forever. [17] This is a final, dramatic event in which Jesus removes sin from Earth forever.

God's judgment

After Satan is removed, all the dead are raised to face God's judgment, as spelled out in these verses:

> "Then I saw a great white throne and him who was seated on it. The earth and the heavens fled from his presence, and there was no place for them. And I saw the dead, great and small, standing before the throne, and books were opened. Another book was opened, which is the Book of Life. The dead were judged according to what they had done as recorded in the books. The sea gave up the dead that were in it, and death and Hades gave up the dead that were in them, and each person was judged according to what they had done. Then death and Hades were thrown into the lake of fire. The lake of fire is the second death. Anyone whose name was not found written in the Book of Life was thrown into the lake of fire." [18]

The person seated on the throne is Jesus. He is both judge and jury for executing God's judgment. The dead who are raised at this point are those who rejected or ignored Jesus during their lifetimes. They will be judged according to their deeds, and none of them will measure up to God's requirements. This is because all of them, including those who were good people while they were on Earth, rejected Jesus as the Son of God and their Savior. Because of this, their names were not recorded in the Book of Life. This judgment is final, and these people will spend eternity in the lake of fire (hell). There are no provisions for an appeal, a last minute change of heart, excuses, blame, or any other ways to avoid this punishment. Please don't be deceived when these verses say that "the dead were judged according to what they had done". The only deed that matters is whether your name is written in the Book of Life. You can only avoid this judgment by accepting Jesus!

It doesn't matter if you are a good person who has done good works. Likewise, it does not matter if you think you are a Christian but have never really accepted Jesus. The only deed that matters is whether you accepted Jesus as your Savior. If you rejected or ignored Jesus, then you are condemned. Jesus has been given full authority by God to execute this judgment at the end times.

Conclusion

The events we just looked at are clearly the most important events in the end times. A very important question is "where is God during all of this time?" God is in heaven, watching Jesus implement his plans. We can see from this recap that God has delegated *full* authority to Jesus to carry out his plans. This is confirmed by Jesus in Matthew 28:18: "Then Jesus came to them and said, 'All authority in heaven and on earth has been given to me'." The final judgments in the end times will all be brought by Jesus. The final judgment when the dead are raised is the point in time where those who rejected or avoided him will find out that Jesus was the only way to God. The fact that God has given all authority to Jesus means that there is no direct path to God without going through Jesus. This may not seem logical to you, but it is true.

Determining Truth

We have already studied in this book the reasons that the Bible is true and reasons that we should not doubt God. Yet, as we have seen, many people are being deceived and will continue to be deceived until the end comes. Have you read all the scripture in this book and still don't think Satan is real or that heaven is a real place? Are you still under the impression that you can get to heaven by being a good person? I sure hope not.

How do we know that God will do what he says? All we have to do is look at the past. Figure 3 compares the plagues that God sent to Egypt with the ones he will send during the end times:

Figure 3 – Egyptian vs. Tribulation Plagues

Plagues of Egypt	Plagues of the Tribulation
Nile turns to blood (Exodus 7:17)	Seas and rivers turn to blood (Revelation 8:8-9, 16:3)
Frogs (Exodus 8:5)	Sun scorches people (Revelation 16:8)
Gnats (Exodus 8:16)	Earthquakes and natural disasters (Revelation 6:12-17, 8:1-6, 16:17-21)
Flies (Exodus 8:21)	Fire burns one third of the earth (Revelation 8:7)
Death of livestock (Exodus 9:6)	Death of earth's creatures (Revelation 8:8-11, 16:3-4)
Boils (Exodus 9:10)	Painful sores (Revelation 16:2)
Hail (Exodus 9:23)	Hail and earthquakes (Revelation 16:17-21)
Locusts attack plants (Exodus 10:12)	Locusts attack humans (Revelation 9:1-6)
Darkness (Exodus 10:22)	Darkness of sun and moon (Revelation 8:12, 16:10)
Death of firstborn (Exodus 12:29)	Evil spirits kill one third of humans (Revelation 9:13-19)

Through Moses, God told the pharaoh of Egypt to let his people go. Each time, Moses told the pharaoh what God was going to do if he refused. Each time, the pharaoh refused because he didn't believe in God, and he didn't believe that God could or would do the things that Moses warned about. God was true to his word each time. The pharaoh and the people of Egypt suffered because of their denial of God. It was completely obvious to all that the God of Moses was superior to the gods of Egypt. Yet, people still refused to obey God.

Jesus gives a final warning to those who want to offer a different spin on what will happen in the end times: "I warn everyone who hears the words of the prophecy of this book [Revelation]: If anyone adds anything to them, God will add to him the plagues described in this book. And if anyone takes words away from this book of prophecy, God will take away from him his share in the tree of life and in the holy city, which are described in this book." [19] This is a stern warning! All of the prophecies in the Bible have been fulfilled except those relating to the end times. God is going to do *exactly* what he said he would do in the future, just as he has done exactly what he said he would do in the past. There is simply no good reason to doubt this.

In the end times, the plagues will be much larger and more severe than the ones that God brought against the Egyptians. Everyone in the world will see and experience these plagues. God gives us a way out, just like he did with the Egyptians. The way out is to accept his Son Jesus, but many people will refuse to do this for reasons we have already discussed. Do you know people who need to make this decision? Perhaps they would benefit from reading this book.

Are You Ready?

We know that several world religions support the idea of karma – i.e. getting what we deserve. The Bible actually supports the concept of karma, but in a slightly different way. Our karma occurs after we die and enter the spirit world. I am not saying that any of us deserve to be in heaven, because we are all sinners. The only thing we deserve is to be held accountable for our actions and decisions. Thankfully, God saves us through his grace - the fact that we can receive Salvation even though we don't deserve it.

Our decisions control whether we make it to heaven. Jesus says: "Whoever acknowledges me before men, I will also acknowledge him before my Father in heaven. But whoever disowns me before men, I will disown him before my Father in heaven." [20] This statement illustrates the whole point of God's plan of salvation. We have the choice to accept or reject Jesus. Jesus will treat us in accordance with the choice we made. If we reject Jesus, we are rejecting heaven. A lot of people will say they don't deserve to be condemned, but it will be exactly what they earned based on the choices they made.

Deciding that we don't need to trust God and that we can look somewhere else for our spirituality brings its own karma. God is in control and he is going to do things his way. He will make sure that everyone sees his power and glory and knows that he is God. We can adopt alternate beliefs that might help us feel better for a while, but these alternate beliefs will not change what is going to happen in the end times or how we will be treated.

We have looked at a lot of evidence concerning God's plans for the future. Do you have any legitimate reasons not to believe that God is in control and will do exactly what he says? Can you see that the events happening in the world today are pointing toward the end times events that we just reviewed?

Summary

Key points that we identified in this chapter are as follows:

- Satan will be given extra powers during the end times that will allow him to further deceive people.
- Satan will be allowed to perform miracles and heal the Antichrist's fatal wound to deceive people.
- The Antichrist receives his power and authority from Satan.
- The Antichrist will break his covenant with Israel and declare

himself to be God. Those who refuse to worship him will be killed.

- God gives *everyone* a chance for salvation through his Son Jesus, but many will harden their hearts and continue to reject him.
- Each of us will be held accountable for the choices we make, and our rewards or punishment will be in accordance with our choices.
- God is in control, and no humans or evil spirits can change God's plan for the end times.
- The end times will prove once and for all that Jesus is the only way to God.
- We need to accept Jesus while we are alive. There are no second chances after we die.
- Jesus has *all* authority to implement God's plans during the end times.

CHAPTER 11:

Conclusion

The time has come to reach a conclusion regarding the truth about God. Perhaps you feel like Arthur Bloch, who said "A conclusion is the place where you get tired of thinking." [1] Hopefully, you are not tired of thinking yet. If you are, then put this book down for a few days and resume reading it at a later time. We have covered a lot of material so far, and we will recap the key points of the material in this chapter to help you organize your thoughts and decide what you believe. The evidence we have seen so far is sufficient to allow everyone to reach an informed decision.

Here is a recap of some important things we have learned so far:

- America is moving away from God. Each succeeding generation is less dependent upon God. People are ignoring organized religions and looking elsewhere for their spiritual needs instead of turning to God.

- There are many false theories about who God is or even if he exists. These theories are not supported by the truths contained in the Bible.

- People tend to look for things that they *want* to believe in. Pride and other human weaknesses sometimes keep us from recognizing the truth.

- Many people have adopted a form of Christianity that allows them to be just religious enough to be comfortable. Many have rejected submitting to Jesus because they don't want to give up self control.

- We don't know as much as we think we do, and we have a

knowledge deficiency related to the spirit world. These things can hurt our ability to believe God.

- The Bible tells us everything that we need to know about God. There is no need to look elsewhere for answers. The Bible is the true Word of God.

- Jesus says that he is the only way to God, yet only a minority of Christians and none of the non-Christians believe this to be true. Universalism is a popular belief today that is consistent with Satan's agenda.

- New Age theories are becoming popular because they provide spirituality without religion. New Age promotes the concept of self-awareness rather than God-awareness.

- A great spiritual warfare is underway between the forces of good (God, Jesus, the Holy Spirit, and angels) and evil (Satan, the fallen angels, and demons). The battle is over which side each of us will choose.

- There is a big difference between knowing who Jesus is and having a relationship with him.

- In the future, there will be a New World Order consisting of a worldwide government and religion. The leader will be the Antichrist, an instrument of Satan. Many people will be deceived by Satan and the Antichrist.

- God's judgment on mankind will occur during the end times in a period known as the tribulation. Everyone will be forced to choose between Jesus and Satan during this period. Those who reject Jesus will eventually be thrown into the lake of fire (hell) for eternity.

- God has given *all* authority for judgment to his Son Jesus. Jesus' judgment will be based on whether our names are written in the Book of Life. Our works and good behavior cannot provide us with salvation from our sins.

There are many other things I could have listed here, but they all point to the same thing – that God is in control and he is going to do things his way. The outcome of the spiritual war has already been determined, which is that God will defeat evil once and for all. The only thing we can control individually is which side we will choose. We can ignore or deny the Bible, but that won't change what God is going to do. We can pretend that all religions lead to God, but that won't change God's announced plan to save us only through Jesus. You are either lined up with Jesus, or you are against him.

I am guessing that some of you have read this far in the book and you still don't believe God's Word. Let's look at some of the reasons that people are still struggling with trusting God. Perhaps you will see something here that helps you understand why you believe certain things. For those of you who are committed Christians, this information might help you deal with friends and family members who don't share your beliefs. Hopefully, some of the information you have read in this book strengthens your own beliefs and allows you to have better conversations with others.

What Are You Looking For?

We have already seen the evidence that supports the existence of God and the fact that Jesus is his Son who was raised from the dead. Yet there are billions of people in the world who don't believe this. In part, this would be due to how these people have been raised and the cultures that they live in. Also, some of these people have not heard the story of Jesus yet.

What is puzzling to me is the number of people who have left organized religion, or just avoided it entirely, to find their spirituality somewhere else. Does this really make sense? If you wanted to purchase some fruits and vegetables, would you go to a grocery store or to a department store? Of course, you would go to a store where you could actually find what you are looking for! Does it really make sense that someone could find God in a place other than where he actually can be found? Even worse, some of you are still sitting in church pews on Sunday and still don't believe.

We will see shortly that there are lots of reasons that people have left churches. However, many of the reasons that people leave a church can be remedied by just going to a different church. What we need to talk about is a person who leaves a church and leaves organized religion also.

My opinion is this: people are leaving organized religion because it is not providing what they are looking for. In other words, God's message is not something they want to believe in or that they want to hear. For example, we know that only a minority of Christians believe that Jesus is the only way to God. Why don't the rest of Christians believe this? Perhaps they have been influenced by our society's infatuation with being politically correct and not offending anyone. I think it is because they don't want to believe it! Perhaps many Christians know that if they believe this, it will change their image of Jesus and God into something defined by God rather than something they define for themselves. Not only that, it might require them to give up some of their selfish desires. Saying that Jesus is the only way to God is certainly offensive to many people in our society today.

There is another reason that people don't attend church. It is because they are not really looking for God (see Romans 10:11). Some people don't really want to find God because they don't want to be exposed for what they really are. If this describes you, then you are like a person who has a serious disease and doesn't want to go to the doctor. Even though the doctor might be able to cure you, you don't want to hear the bad news.

People have been guilty of making God in their own image for thousands of years. Many of us just don't want to accept absolute truth, which is that God is exactly who he says he is. Instead, we would rather pick and choose what we believe and create a cafeteria religion. This practice has been around for thousands of years, but recently has become epidemic. Let's examine why.

The first influence has been our desires to acquire things that are exactly what we want and get them when we want them. The number of choices we have today is significantly larger than just fifty years ago. Our modern products and conveniences have changed our desires and behavior!

The availability of information has also affected our beliefs. The information choices that are available have expanded considerably. There is information available at our fingertips that just didn't exist fifty years ago. Satan has certainly taken advantage of the Internet to further his agenda. Satan has inspired many people to put their negative or alternative opinions about religion on the Internet. Anyone willing to spend just a few dollars per month can have a web site and fill it with their own opinions. These opinions have influenced people and have given them doubts about their beliefs.

We have taken the concept of making God in our own image and expanded it to make religion in our own image. For some, this means a little bit of Christianity, a few New Age beliefs, perhaps meditation from Buddhism, and a few other things that were just made up by the individual. In most cases, cafeteria religion reduces the importance of God and increases the importance of the individual.

There seems to be a rebellion against the established religions because of one huge issue – they tell you what you need to believe! For some, this is like fingernails scratching on a chalkboard. They will keep looking until they find what they want to believe, and they won't have to look very far. Thanks to the Internet, you can find someone who agrees with you very easily.

God doesn't offer a cafeteria plan for religion. There aren't multiple sources of information about God. The Bible is the one and only Word of God. God doesn't give us multiple descriptions of himself so we can choose which one we like. Please remember that your choices have long term consequences.

We have known for two thousand years that people would start moving away from God as we got closer to the end times. We know that because of God's warning that we saw in an earlier chapter that men will not put up with sound doctrine but will gather around them teachers who say what they want to hear, to suit their selfish desires. [2] It is part of our human nature to look out for ourselves, but we have taken this tendency to the extreme. The problem with this approach is a failure to acknowledge the truth. Nothing we believe can change the truth because the truth comes from our Creator. We can't find the truth unless we are actually looking for it. We can't look for the truth unless we look to God himself. We can't believe the truth unless we give up our selfish desires. And, we can't give up our selfish desires until we acknowledge that God's plans for us are so much better than anything we could come up with on our own.

The statistics that we looked at earlier in this book reveal that many of the people who have beliefs about God that are contrary to the Bible are still calling themselves Christians and are still attending church. If you are one of these people, perhaps you are in a church that doesn't teach you everything you should know about the Bible. On the other hand, maybe you are just ignoring the things you hear that you don't want to believe, or you just think that these things don't really apply to you (a real danger since many people blame all their problems on someone else). Attending church will not make you a Christian, just like sitting in a garage will not make you a car. God knows your heart and is not fooled by outward appearances.

I have known Christians who view their Christianity as an insurance policy. Once they accept Jesus, they feel that their eternal life is secure, so they back to doing whatever they want in their current life. Some of these people continue to attend church, and some don't, but they all have the same attitude. This attitude is that Jesus only came to provide eternal life after we die, and that he has no relevance to our lives on Earth. Perhaps you know some people like this also, and they could be a major reason that you don't see any need to become a Christian or attend a church. These people have totally missed the point. Jesus also came to show us how to live. He wants us to glorify God, obey his commands, and do his work here on Earth. Keep this in mind - we do not invite Jesus into our lives. Instead, he invites us into his life! By joining him and following him, we become happier in this life and more prepared for the next one.

Reasons for Rejecting Christianity

Since this book is being written from a Christian perspective, we will focus in this section on why people are rejecting Christianity (including those who still call themselves Christian but aren't really Christians at all). Specifically, we need to look at why Christians are leaving organized religion to find their spirituality somewhere else. As we saw earlier in this book, there has been significant growth in the un-churched population in the United States since the early 1990s. In addition, there has been an increase in the number of Christians who don't attend church or take their religion very seriously. These numbers tell us that many people just don't consider God to be relevant or important in our modern society. We already know about the desire people have to define their own God, but what else is going on? Sadly, we will see that many of the reasons for rejecting Christianity relate to the behavior of Christians! A person who wrote to the editor of the Atlanta Journal-Constitution recently said "I really like Jesus. It is his fan club that I am not too wild about."

Objections to Christianity

The objections in this section are summarized from a variety of publicly available surveys.

Christians are too judgmental. This opinion goes hand-in-hand with the opinion that there are too many rules in the Christian faith. It is true that in the past there were many sermons preached on the "thou shalt not" theme. If you have ever been in a church youth group, you know that at least once per year someone would tell you about the evils of sex, drugs, and alcohol. When I was a teenager, there were still churches that condemned dancing. All of these things create the perception that Christians only want to talk about things that are considered sinful.

I am fortunate to be in a church that focuses on how we can become more like Jesus. The church has a much more positive approach to life by showing you how to act rather than focusing on how not to act. Jesus is the best role model who ever lived. If we focus on him, we tend to be less negative.

It is part of our human nature to be judgmental, in spite of God's warnings about being this way. Isn't a person who thinks that Christians are too judgmental being judgmental also? Perhaps it would be more useful to help each other avoid this negative behavior. Is it valid to not believe in Jesus because we don't want to hear that we are sinners? I don't think so. The Bible tells us that we are all born as sinners, whether we want to acknowledge it or not. You don't become a Christian to be condemned, but to be saved. The Bible tells us: "For God did not send his Son into the world to condemn the world, but to save the world through him." [3]

If you think that there are too many rules in Christianity, let me remind you that Jesus saves us by grace, not by works. All we need to do to become a Christian is to acknowledge that we are sinners and ask Jesus to forgive us. There isn't a list of rules that we need to obey to take advantage of the salvation provided by Jesus. We will find that after we have a personal relationship with Jesus, we will want to be more like him.

Christians think that Jesus is the only way to God. This belief is called exclusivity, and it implies that Christians have a "holier than thou" attitude. To say that Jesus is the only way to God is offensive to all other religions, and most people in today's world (including many people who call themselves Christian) don't believe it is based on the truth. Why would anyone want to go to church and associate with people who have this attitude? The problem, of course, with exclusivity is that Christians didn't make this up. They are simply reporting what Jesus said about himself. Therefore, if anyone disagrees with this belief, their issue is with Jesus himself rather than the Christians who believe that Jesus tells the truth.

Many religions are more tolerant than Christianity in terms of believing that there are multiple ways to God. However, the bottom line is that most people think that whatever they believe currently is correct – that is why they believe it. If you felt that your current beliefs were not correct, you would change them! If anyone rejects Christianity because of the belief in exclusivity, it would reveal a focus on self rather than a focus on Jesus. God did not send Jesus to create some sort of exclusive religion that would offend people. He sent Jesus to create salvation for *everyone*. This was God's way of trying to save us from the consequences of our sins.

Christians are intolerant. What does intolerance really mean? It really means that a person is not willing to listen to anyone else's beliefs. Christians were instructed by Jesus to spread the good news about his saving grace. If a

Christian tells someone else about Jesus, does this mean the Christian is not tolerant? On the contrary, the person who is not tolerant could be the one whom the Christian is talking with. Many people just don't want to hear anything about Jesus, and unwillingness to listen is the definition of intolerance. However, the vast majority of Christians that I know are willing to listen to what other people believe. They may not agree with these beliefs, but they are willing to listen. If a person thinks that Christians are intolerant, then it is likely that the person himself is intolerant. Jesus said "Why do you look at the speck of sawdust in your brother's eye and pay no attention to the plank in your own eye?" 4

You can't take the Bible literally, and it is too old to be relevant. There is also the belief that the Bible, especially the New Testament, was just a bunch of made up stories designed to make us follow a man-defined God. We already talked about how we know the Bible is true, and I am not going to repeat all those arguments here. If any of you are still unsure about this, go back and read that chapter again. I believe that the Bible is God's Word, written by people whom he inspired. The overall consistency of the books of the Bible points to a master author (God) who oversaw the entire development of the Bible. In addition, there is a perspective in the Bible that could only have come from the one who can view the future.

To those who believe that something as old as the Bible can't be relevant, I would ask this question: When does something cease to be relevant? Does a book have a useful life of five years, twenty years, or a hundred years? Where is the cutoff? If there is a cutoff, why do our schools still study books such as *The Iliad* and *The Odyssey* that are older than many portions of the Bible? The answer is that a book's relevance is not related to its age. Certain books, such as the Bible, are timeless because of their subject matter. This means that they make sense to any generation.

Having said that, it is apparent that some of the examples used in the Bible were appropriate to the timeframe in which they were written. No reasonable person would take these literally after studying the context in which they were written. For example, Paul told women that they should not wear makeup. This message was given to an audience that associated heavy makeup with pagan temple prostitutes. Today, there are few people who take Paul's advice literally. Please remember that many things in the Bible make more sense when viewing them in the context in which they were written.

The Bible is not believable. This is the belief that there are just too many "fairy tales" in the Bible – things that a logical person just could not accept. We talked about this in the chapter on getting out of the box of small thinking. If anyone says that the Bible is not believable, this certainly indicates a lack of faith in God. The Bible says that nothing is impossible for God, and who are we to argue with this? If God is the Creator of the universe, human and plant life, and all of the other wonders of nature, wouldn't anything else be pretty simple for him? As we discussed earlier, we actually have a limited knowledge of science and an even more limited knowledge of the spirit world. We need to swallow our pride and accept the fact that God can do whatever he wants to.

I don't want anyone telling me what to do. This is a common objection to Christianity by those who don't want to give up control of their lives. When we were growing up, we tended to rebel against our parents and question why they had so many rules. We failed to realize that our parents had rules for our own benefit, so we rejoiced when we were free from this burden.

Having this attitude toward Christianity means that we are failing to understand that God wants to save us from ourselves. His plans for us are so much better than ours, yet many people do not trust him enough to ever find out what those plans are. I can give you a hint in this area based on my own experience. If you are not happy (meaning experiencing joy rather than temporary pleasures), then you are probably not following God's plan. The reason that God doesn't bless us more than he does is because we don't let him! We are either too busy trying to tell him what to do for us, or ignoring him completely. If we just ask God to bless us in any way that he chooses, we would all be surprised at the results. Our attempts to make God and Jesus into servants for us are just not working.

Recently, a friend of mine told me that he was not a Christian. Normally, this would not be a surprise except that this friend was active in my church and had been attending there for many years. He told me that he had been faking being a Christian his entire adult life. Recently, some changes in his life convinced him that he needed to deal with becoming a Christian. He knew that it was the right thing to do and that he would be headed to hell unless he accepted Jesus into his heart. However, something in his heart was preventing him from making the right decision. He indicated that perhaps the issue of control was one thing that was preventing him from accepting Jesus. After he described his life to me, I could tell that control was a big issue.

If you think you have control over your life, you have been fooled by Satan. Everything you have belongs to God, and he can take any or all of it away at any time. You are just operating under the illusion that you have control. If you are like my friend, please pray that God will remove your selfishness so that you can enjoy the blessings that he will give you through having a relationship with Jesus.

I have doubts about God. I will bet that most of us reached a point in our lives where we questioned if everything we heard and read about God was true. Unfortunately, many atheists and agnostics are former Christians. However, we are also seeing former atheists who became Christians after attempting to disprove the existence of God. I believe that these doubts about God come from Satan. So, what can we do when these doubts arise? First of all, we can talk with other Christian believers and with church staff members. Many of these people have gone through the same experience. Second, we can read the Bible and find additional books that explain more about God. Third, we can pray that God will help us answer our questions.

In any case, deciding to avoid God or his church just because you have doubts about him doesn't seem to be beneficial. We are more likely to get the answers we need while participating in church activities than we are by ignoring God completely. We need to be constantly aware that Satan is a liar and a deceiver. He would like nothing better than to see someone give up on Christianity. He will make alternative religions sound more attractive by appealing to each person's individual weaknesses. He will put thoughts into our heads that will confuse us and cause us to act in an irrational manner. Doubts about God are caused by Satan, and we can only protect ourselves from Satan by allowing God to protect us.

Objections to Organized Religion

We can learn from several studies that church attendance in America declined steadily from the 1950s to the 1990s. Since the 1990s, attendance has been stable but has not grown very much. We also looked at a survey earlier in this book that revealed people are leaving organized religions to look for spirituality elsewhere. One 2006 survey that examined why people left churches reveals some interesting statistics: [5]

- 59 percent left because of changes in their life situation
- 19 percent of these got too busy to attend church
- 17 percent had conflicts between church, family and home responsibilities
- 17 percent moved too far from the church
- 15 percent had work situations that prevented attendance
- 12 percent left after getting divorced or separated
- 37 percent became disenchanted with the pastor or the church members
- 26 percent said the church was not fulfilling their needs
- 22 percent changed their beliefs or attitudes about church

I would interpret "changes in life situation" to mean that these people found something that they would rather spend time on. Perhaps it was golfing, going to the lake, sleeping late, working in the garden, or whatever. When someone says he is too busy to attend church, it means that he would rather spend time on his outside activities. For those people who said they moved too far away, got divorced, became disenchanted with the pastor or the members, and said the church did not meet their needs, I have some simple advice: Find a different church! Yet, the survey revealed that most of these people are not actively looking for one.

For those who were disenchanted, the most common specifics mentioned were that church members were hypocritical and too judgmental. In other words, the members are driving people away rather than the pastor. This is a warning to all of us who are Christians and regular church attendees! The church is full of sinners because we are *all* sinners. If anyone thinks there are hypocrites and sinners in church, they are correct! Is this really a good reason to not attend? Can you name one place on Earth where you can go and not associate with sinners or people who are hypocritical or judgmental?

This same survey found that approximately 80 percent of those who left did not have a strong belief in God, expressing the opinion that work and family are a higher priority. However, almost all of those who left did profess to have *some* belief in God.[6] This raises the question of whether the lack of strong belief caused them to leave church or occurred after they left church. I think we could say that leaving church would not do anything to strengthen a belief in God unless that church was teaching something contrary to the Bible. Likewise, if a person did not have a strong belief in God, they probably wouldn't have been going to church anyway. Frankly, a lot of the reasons for leaving a church just sound like excuses rather than reasons to leave.

Here are some additional complaints that are often voiced about organized religion:

Church is boring and/or I don't fit there. If you don't feel that you are in the right church, then find a different church. Today, there are worship styles that go from ceremonial to traditional to completely contemporary. You can find different preaching styles, dress codes, building configuration, and almost anything else you would be more comfortable with. The important point is to find a church where the Word of God is preached. By that, I mean that you should make sure that the pastor reads from the Bible and explains the meaning of the Bible and its application to our daily lives.

For the younger generation, social influences seem to be important in choosing a church. In my generation, young people went out on dates.

Today, young people just "hang out" a lot. If this is important to you, find a church that has people you wouldn't mind hanging out with. Many people think that Christians are boring, but this is far from the truth. My best friends are Christians. These people are just not like the friends you meet at work or through your community. These are the people who would give you an organ transplant if you needed it, who will pick you up when you are down, and who you can trust without hesitation. Life is not complete unless you have friends like this, and the best place to find them is in a Bible-believing church.

Churches are full of hypocrites. This is absolutely true. These people are sinners who look righteous on Sunday and then act just like non-Christians during the week. Why would anyone want to associate with people like this? The answer is because they need our help. They are no different than any other sinner. They need to be in church to get the help they need. Perhaps it will dawn on them some day that there is a difference in what they say and how they act. What they don't realize is that their actions keep other people away from our churches. I am sure that if you have a job you are probably working with hypocrites. Are you willing to quit your job so you won't have to associate with these people? Are you willing to put up with hypocrites during the week but not on Sunday? Are you comparing yourself to someone who isn't a very good role model? If so, compare yourself to Jesus. He is the one who has set the standard for behavior that is pleasing to God.

If a person stays away from church to avoid sinners, then what type of people is that person associating with outside of the church? People criticized Jesus because he associated with sinners. His response was: "It is not the healthy who need a doctor, but the sick." [7] There are two types of sinners: those who don't realize or care that they are sinners, and those who are trying to deal with their sin. If a person wants help on dealing with sin, they can find it inside the church and by reading God's Word. If you are a Christian, have you let God change your behavior?

Churches are too involved in politics and social issues. If you took out the word "too," this would be a true statement. Churches have definitely become involved in political and social issues. My question is: what is wrong with this? Jesus spoke about political and social issues. Look at the number of groups that have been formed to push specific agendas, especially those that promote agendas which are contrary to the Bible. Someone needs to speak for God on these issues, and there is no better representative than God's churches and God's people. I think part of the negative perception here is that people think that the churches have some sort of hidden agenda such as obtaining preferential tax breaks. This is just not true for the churches that I am familiar with. Churches are speaking out on issues of importance and are asking us to vote for political candidates whose positions are consistent with God's. I hope we never reach the point in our democracy where God's people are not allowed to express views about important issues for our daily lives.

Preachers are only interested in money. I read a book recently where the author continually blasted clergy members for asking for money. His impression was that the only thing that mattered to them was having bigger budgets, bigger buildings, bigger salaries, and more staff. Perhaps there are people like this, but is it fair to say that the clergy in general is like this? Sure, there have been some TV preachers who have given religion a bad name because of their extravagant lifestyles, but not all TV preachers are money oriented, and many of them are bringing messages that need to be heard. This is also true for the leaders of your local churches. There may be some who get misguided occasionally, but the vast majority of them are trying to serve God. It is not valid to reject God because of the negative image being portrayed by a few highly visible preachers.

It is not important to attend church. It is true that someone can be a Christian and not attend church. God's definition of church is the body of believers (not the building or local congregation). So being a Christian automatically makes us part of the body of believers. However, not attending church hurts our ability to grow as Christians. We also would miss out on the ability to help others who could use our support, as well as our ability to receive support and prayers from other believers. For anyone who wants to live up to God's expectations, attending church is the best way to begin to fulfill those expectations.

I am a member of a church that is defying the negative trends we have been talking about. The membership is growing, additional services keep being added, and increasing numbers of people are becoming involved in mission work and other service for God. It is obvious that this church is drawing people who are hungry for God.

Why are churches like this able to succeed when others are struggling? First of all, there is strong leadership at the top. The pastor preaches from the Bible and explains it so that everyone can understand. This fulfills the desire that people have to learn more about God. Second, there is something for everyone. There are different worship styles in different facilities. Members are able to pick and choose to suit their personal preferences. However, the same Bible-based message is preached in all services. Third, the church's mission statement is clearly articulated and is followed by the members. The mission statement includes loving God, worshiping God, and reaching people for Jesus Christ.

Are there hypocrites in this church? Of course there are. Is the church involved in political or social issues? Yes, when appropriate. Is this church perfect? No, this is not a perfect church because there is no such thing.

If you are a person who is making excuses for not attending church, think about why you feel this way and whether you can change these feelings. Think about the things that you would rather do instead of attending church, and then think about these things from God's perspective. If you are not involved with a church, then you may not spending enough time with God.

Why We Can't Redefine God

The practice of cafeteria religion is simply an attempt to redefine God. The driving force behind cafeteria religion is the desire by a person to believe what he wants to, which not only redefines God but labels him as a liar. This just doesn't make sense! There are certainly lots of reasons to accept God's Word as being true, but I can give you the best one right now – your life depends on it.

Based on everything you have read so far in this book, can you honestly say that God is not relevant for your life? When you see events happening that were predicted in the Bible two thousand years ago, doesn't this indicate that God is in control of our future? If heaven and hell are real (which they are), and God's statements are true (which they are), then each of us is faced with a choice of eternal life or eternal damnation. Jesus, the Son of God, can provide us with eternal life. That fact alone makes God relevant. Accepting Jesus is the most important decision that you need to make in your lifetime.

We have seen a huge interest in spirituality in our modern world, yet people are not turning to God to meet their spirituality needs. Doesn't it make sense that we should go directly to the source of all spirituality to get our needs met? Isn't God the "highest and best" source of information? Isn't any information that is not from God coming from Satan? Let's recap some of the information we have covered in this book that points to why we can't redefine God.

We have human limitations. We have more information than we have ever had in the history of mankind, but we still don't know everything. Our perspective is limited, and certainly it is not as comprehensive as God's. In spite of our limitations, we have a tendency to become prideful. Our pride causes many people to think that they are as smart or smarter than God, and therefore causes them to think they don't need God. In addition to pride, our human nature makes it difficult to accept God because some of the things that God says and does are just not logical. Furthermore, we tend to look for things we want to believe, and believing in Christianity requires us to give up self control. All of these things together make it difficult for many people to accept God. Accordingly, many people just choose portions of the Bible to believe in so they can define their own God. Does this mean that our cafeteria religion is acceptable to God? On the contrary, it means that we need God even more to help us make up for our human weaknesses. Only God can restrain Satan so that he does not take advantage of these weaknesses. Only God can open our eyes to the truth. Only God can provide us with the ability to discern between good and evil. Only God can help us overcome our individual weaknesses to see clearly that he is in control.

Most people believe in heaven, but many don't know how to get there. We see people today looking in all kinds of places for their spiritual and religious needs. When people move away from God like this, it reveals human weaknesses. God has answers for everything we are looking for. Only God can tell us how to get to heaven and allow us to experience heaven on Earth through his blessings.

God is the Creator of the universe. We know this because God tells us himself. Even the evil spirits acknowledge God's awesome power. We should not make the mistake of limiting God based on the image of him that we want to believe. A Creator that could make the massive universe that we live in and design the details down to the smallest atom in the smallest creature is surely capable of things we can't even imagine. The Bible tells us that nothing is impossible for God, yet many people still don't believe this. There is no more awesome force in the universe than God. There is no one more worthy of worship than God. We are living in his creation, which was designed and built based on his rules. We are like tenants who are temporarily using his possessions. He made our world and he can change it anytime he wants to. He created humanity and each of us. God is our Father, and we are made in his image. None of us would be alive today if it were not for the actions of God.

God hasn't changed. God is the same yesterday, today, and tomorrow. The Bible contains amazing consistency in showing us who God is and how he is implementing his plan for the world. Those who think that God needs to change because the Bible was written 2,000 years ago need to realize that God is not subject to our dimension of time. He was able to influence the biblical writers to bring a message that is timeless. We are the ones who changed in the last two thousand years, not God. God represents truth for any generation in the past, present, or future.

We are born with a sin nature which separates us from God. I realize that quite a few of you don't believe you were born with a sin nature. God makes it clear that he doesn't agree with this opinion. Many of our modern gurus would like us to believe there is no such thing as sin. This theory is the ultimate deception by Satan – i.e. Satan saying that he doesn't really exist. Satan knows that if there is no sin, then there is no need for Jesus. However, the Bible tells us that we have a sin nature that has existed since Adam and Eve disobeyed God. A sin nature means that we are born as sinners, separated from God. This is true even before we are able to commit any sinful acts.

God is sinless and perfect. None of us can possibly measure up to him, and we certainly can't become equal to him by improving our consciousness or by performing good works. We can never obtain perfection, but we can obtain forgiveness. God is important to each of us because we need to be reconciled with him individually. Each of us needs to be reconciled to God so we will no longer be separated from him and so we can spend eternity with him after we die. God teaches us that this reconciliation is complete when Jesus forgives us for our sins. Another person cannot make you a Christian! Accepting Jesus' death on the cross as atonement for sin is an action that each one of us must take on our own. You cannot be born into this world as a Christian, but you can leave this world as a Christian.

Satan is a liar and deceiver who is trying to keep us away from God. We spent a lot of time looking at Satan in this book because I felt that it was important for everyone to see how much influence he has in our modern world. Satan, evil spirits, and demons are real and are more active today than ever. Satan has contradicted or counterfeited almost all of the basic principles of the Christian faith. He has enlisted the help of demons and rebellious angels to help keep us away from God. He appears to be influencing the minds of many false prophets who have shown up lately as predicted in the Bible. Satan is a powerful force who has lots of help.

God provides the guidelines that we need for recognizing Satan's work and resisting the temptation to believe in some of the new theories about God that Satan's representatives have proposed. Satan has also destroyed much of our morality and is working on replacing our governments. God is more important now than ever before because Satan has increased his attacks, and they are coming from new directions. God can help us recognize and avoid the things that come from Satan.

We cannot resist Satan without God. God is important because Satan is a spirit, and we cannot fight a spiritual war. The forces of good and evil are fighting for control over your spirit and your mind. Only God can represent us in this war, and only God can actually win this war. Satan's defeat is certain. We are not strong enough on our own to resist Satan. He makes things appealing and attractive, and many times we don't realize that he is behind a temptation that we give in to. Furthermore, the Bible tells us that the Holy Spirit is currently restraining Satan. This means that if we are Christian, we have extra protection against Satan from the Holy Spirit. In the end times, the restraints on Satan will be released. If we are alive at that time, we will be required to worship the Antichrist, or we will be killed. God will be needed to help us through this time so that we do not act foolishly.

Only Jesus can save us from the consequences of sin. God came to the earth in human form through his Son Jesus. The death and resurrection of Jesus means that he suffered the consequences of sin (which is death) on our behalves. Christianity is the only religion that supports the fact that Jesus is the Son of God and our Savior. God has given full authority to Jesus, and we are accountable to Jesus for our choices. He will judge us based on whether our names are written in the Book of Life, not based on our works or any other reasons we think that we deserve to be in heaven. When we look at Jesus, we see God.

Occasionally, I hear people say that they just don't need God. What they really mean is that everything is going well for them *right now*. They are healthy, have money, have a nice house and possessions and a good family, they like their job, and have no real issues to deal with. This type of attitude shows a very narrow perspective of focusing on the short term and ignoring the long term. There is no acknowledgement that they are all sinners regardless of their current life situation. Only Jesus can fix this.

Most people believe that there are many ways get to God. While this theory may seem to be common sense, there are problems with it. First,

God does not tell us this anywhere in the Bible. Second, Jesus himself says that he is the only way to God. And Third, God tells us that *all* authority for judgment has been given to Jesus. The Bible tells us that many will show up for the final judgment and Jesus will tell them: "I never knew you. Away from me..." [8] Jesus is saying that just because we know him, or know who he is, that he doesn't necessarily know us. He only knows us when we accept him as our Savior and do God's will. These things make Jesus necessary for our modern world.

The Bible is the true Word of God. When we talked about the search for truth, we focused on why we know the Bible contains the true Word of God. The Bible is our written record of God's actions, promises, and covenant with his people. The Bible is a great historical document, but it is much more. It tells us everything we need to know about God and his Son Jesus. It tells us about the afterlife that we can experience by accepting Jesus' gift of salvation. It tells us things about the spirit world that we could only learn from someone who has actually been there. It provides guidelines for us in how we should live and relate to our fellow man. It contains wisdom that is timeless, prophecies that always come true, and hope for our future. Many books contain alternate theories about spirituality and religion, but these books cannot claim the same authorship as the Bible. Only the Bible gives us the criteria for deciding which other books contain truth.

If we reject Jesus, he will reject us. We have seen that God has given full authority to Jesus to judge. Jesus tells us that if we accept him, then he will accept us. If we reject him, then he will reject us. This means that Jesus holds the key to our life after death. Whether we end up in heaven or hell depends on decisions we make while we are alive. Many people fail to realize that not accepting Jesus means that we are rejecting him. Remaining neutral or not sure, or just putting off a decision means that we are rejecting him. God has made this decision easy for us when we examine all of the evidence. It is never too late for us to make this decision while we are alive. It is comforting to know that no matter how bad we are or what we have done in our lifetimes, God is waiting on us to turn to him. When we ask Jesus if he will save us, the answer is always yes. He loves us the same way that we love our own children – unconditionally.

Summary

America is a very prosperous nation. Our standards of living provide us with many things that we don't actually need. We tend to get comfortable with these things and assume that we are doing fine without God. What is really happening is that we build comfort zones that give us a false sense of security and control. Perhaps the recent financial crisis has taught us that we shouldn't get too comfortable with material things.

I believe the evidence in this book points out that we need God more than ever. There are more threats from the evil forces than ever before. If we are alive when the tribulation begins, we will probably lose most of the things that we now own. At some point in our lives, each of us will have to deal with the death of a loved one, serious illness, job loss, a natural disaster, or other traumatic events. Where are we going to turn for support and comfort? Is obtaining a higher level of consciousness going to help us get through these tough times? Is meditation going to help you get over the loss of a loved one or enable you to see that person in heaven? We can only turn to God for support and comfort, and he is patiently waiting on us. He has already issued the invitation, and it is up to us to accept it.

What Do You Believe?

I believe that most of the people reading this book will be Christians or people who think they are a Christian. Regardless of whether you are a Christian, let me ask you a question. What do you believe? Try to put yourself into to one of these categories:

- I am a Christian who has a relationship with Jesus. I attend a church regularly and I am striving to become more like Jesus.
- I am a Christian, but Christianity is not an important priority in my life right now. I attend church occasionally or not at all. I don't really know that much about the Bible.
- I grew up in a Christian environment, but I moved away when I became an adult.

- I am not a Christian. I believe in some sort of God, but I am still looking for answers.
- I am an atheist or agnostic.

I realize that you may not fit exactly into one of these groups, so pick the closest one. Let's talk about things you do to move from one group to another.

If you are a Christian who has a relationship with Jesus, congratulations! You may have found this book to contain mostly material that you are already familiar with. You may have learned something about some of the things happening today that are pulling people away from God. I hope you can share this book with those that you know who are struggling with their belief in God. There is probably more scripture quoted in this book than what many of these people have read. Most of our young people are now being exposed to these alternate theories about God, and they need our guidance to sort out the truth.

If you are a Christian who isn't really giving your Christianity much attention, what would it take to get you to do so? Have you learned anything about God by reading this book? Have you learned anything about yourself while reading this book? I know many people who fall into this category. For most of them, their career, hobbies, and family responsibilities take priority over their religion. Many are dedicated to finding what the world considers to be success. Even if you are doing a good job in these areas, are you becoming the type of person that God wants you to be? Are you sure that you are going to heaven? Do you have any valid excuses for not giving God the attention that he deserves? Have you decided that there must be many paths to God? Have you "put on the full armor of God" to be able to discern the truth or do you fit into the "comfortable Christian" group?

If you are a person who used to be a Christian but have given up on it during your adult life, you are not alone. There are large numbers of people in this group. Perhaps you rebelled against your parents, or you ran into someone who convinced you that there is no God. Perhaps, like many, you had a bad experience while you were in a church. Perhaps you think Christianity is just old fashioned and no longer relevant. Perhaps you like the ability to define your own God. Or, maybe you never really believed in the first place and just went to church because your parents made you go. If so, are you sure that you have been saved? Do you feel that your life is complete, or is there something missing? Do you feel that you are going to heaven? Are you being fair to your family by ignoring God and perhaps keeping them away from God at the same time? I don't really know your situation, but I know that God is real, and I know what he has done for me. I hope you will reconsider your beliefs and take the time to get more information and talk with people who can explain the things that you might have doubts about.

If you are not a Christian, then I want to thank you for reading this book. I told you up front that this book would be written from a Christian perspective, and I realize that you may not be interested in a Christian perspective. Perhaps you only read this book to find some things you could argue with. Perhaps the book wasn't what you were looking for, but I hope it gave you some things to think about. In the next section, I will tell you how to get additional information.

For all of you - if you knew with one hundred percent certainty that Jesus was the only way to God, what changes would you need to make in your life and your beliefs to make sure that you don't miss out on the opportunity that Jesus gives to us? How do you think Jesus feels about those who don't really believe what he said? How do you think Jesus feels about those who don't pay attention to him and don't obey his commands? Are you secure in your own beliefs but are ignoring the needs of others? When you finish reading this book, are you just going to put it on the shelf and forget about it? These are questions that we should all think about.

Do you want to talk about what you have read in this book? Look for my Facebook page or visit my web site at www.AreYouWrongAboutGod.com. My web site contains a blog where you will have the opportunity to ask questions or make comments on the important subject matter contained in this book. Please share these sites with others who would benefit from the subject matter in this book.

Next Steps

Sometimes, we make bad decisions. In life, some of our mistakes can be corrected, and some can't. A good analogy is the game of golf. I love playing golf, but I am just not that good. Perhaps I need to spend more time actually trying to get better! One thing certain about golf is that every golfer at some point is going to hit a really bad shot. When this happens, it is always the golfer's fault - there is no one else to blame it on! The really good golfers have learned how to forget about their last shot because they know that the only important shot is their next one. The average golfer, like me, remembers the last shot while trying to hit the next one. When doing this, it creates a tendency to overreact. For example, if the last shot sliced off to the right, the golfer's next shot may go to the left because he is trying to correct for his last mistake. Once you hit a bad shot, it can't be corrected!

The good news that Jesus brings is that he will forgive us for our sins and mistakes regardless of what they were or whether they were correctable. He accepts us with open arms regardless of all the baggage and unworthiness that we bring. If you have been ignoring Jesus, this is a correctable mistake! The most important thing becomes what you do next, not what you did previously.

If you are not a Christian, perhaps you are interested in becoming one or learning more about Christianity. Becoming a Christian is fairly simple as explained in John 3:16: "For God so loved the world that he gave his one and only Son, that whoever believes in him shall not perish but have eternal life." The only requirement is that you believe with your heart that Jesus is the Son of God and that God raised him from the dead. If you really believe in Jesus in your heart and you ask him to come into your life, you will receive the gift of the Holy Spirit from God. The Holy Spirit will give you the desire to learn more about Jesus and to be more like him. Place your trust in God's Word, the Bible, rather than a set of man-made rules about what you must do to be saved.

Here are some suggested steps for avoiding the deceptions we have talked about in this book:

- Get away from Satan. What does this mean? It means to study God's Word to help you identify things that you should avoid. Remember that the definition of sin is anything that separates you from God. The popular phrase "What would Jesus do?" is a pretty good phrase to remember when you are making decisions.

- Avoid the false prophets. This one is pretty easy. Don't read books that pull you away from God. If there are people on television who you feel are leading you away from God, then don't watch those shows. Remember that people who do not acknowledge that Jesus is the Son of God are false prophets. People who support the theory that there are many ways to God may be trying to pull you away from the truth. Focus on books and shows that help you understand the Bible!

- Go to church. The church of Jesus is not a building, but rather a body of believers. It is important for Christians to be part of a body of believers. You will hear God's Word and learn how to put it into action. When times get tough, your Christian friends will support you, and you can support them. You can find a church where you will feel like you belong if you just take the time to look for it.

- Hang out with the right people. If your friends or co-workers are pulling you away from God or distracting you from God, then perhaps it is time to change who you are associating with. Think about joining a small group of Christian believers who will help you learn more about God.

- Read your Bible. I probably referenced less than one-tenth of one percent of the Bible in this book. There is much more Scripture that is worthy of your time. Studying the Bible *always* improves your understanding of God.

- Spend quiet time with God. Quiet time is important because it enables us to eliminate distractions and focus on God. This is a good time for listening to God. The only way we can effectively listen to God is to quit trying to tell him what to do.

Help Spread the Word

I had a number of reasons for writing this book, but the most important one is that I feel a sense of urgency to get the truth about Christianity to those who are ignoring it or drifting away. In particular, I think the trends we are seeing in the United States are very disturbing. Writing a book allows this message to get to thousands of people instead of just the few that I could contact personally. Because I feel that this is such an important topic, I have decided to donate most of the proceeds of this book to Christian charities. Your purchase of this book enables me to contribute much more to Christian causes than I could do with my limited retirement income.

There are many worthy charities that are spreading the great news about Christianity throughout the world. One of my favorites is Right From The Heart, based in Marietta, Georgia. This is a unique ministry whose mission is to spread the message of Christianity through the media. The ministry rents time on secular radio and television stations to bring easily understood messages about God to people who are stuck in traffic, watching the news, or going about their daily routines. The goal is to reach people who are not attending church and are not watching or listening to Christian broadcasts. Through the use of the Internet, email, and other technologies, the ministry is now reaching out to people throughout the world. I would recommend that you check out their web site at www.rightfromtheheart.org. On this site, you can sign up for a free daily devotional message to be delivered to your email address, listen to excellent Bible-based teaching by founder Bryant Wright, follow them on Facebook, make a contribution, and participate in an Internet prayer ministry (www.rightfromtheknees.org). There are many other ministries that deserve your support as well.

When I graduated from college, the college president spoke at my graduation. He asked us to talk about the college to everyone we met and to spread the good word about what a great school it was. Then, he advised us to "put your money where your mouth is". (He was a good fundraiser!). This same advice applies to Christianity. Please talk about it, and then put your money where your mouth is. You can make a difference in someone's life!

Remember that Jesus has commanded each one of us to spread the good news that he brings. "Therefore go and make disciples of all nations, baptizing them in the name of the Father and of the Son and of the Holy Spirit, and teaching them to obey everything I have commanded you. And surely I am with you always, to the very end of the age." (Matthew 28:19-20)

BIBLIOGRAPHY AND NOTES

Preface

1 Barna Group. "Casual Christians and the Future of America." http://www.barna.org/barna-update/article/13-culture/268-casual-christians-and-the-future-of-america. Copyright © by The Barna Group, Ltd.

2 Ephesians 6:11-12. All scripture quotations, unless otherwise indicated, are taken from the *Holy Bible, New International Version*®. *NIV*®. Copyright © 1973, 1978, 1984 by International Bible Society. Used by permission of Zondervan. All rights reserved.

Introduction

1 Barna, George. *The Frog In The Kettle*. Regal Books, 1990.

2 Barna Group. "Casual Christians and the Future of America." http://www.barna.org/barna-update/article/13-culture/268-casual-christians-and-the-future-of-america. Copyright © by The Barna Group, Ltd. Also "Americans Are Exploring New Ways of Experiencing God." http://www.barna.org/barna-update/article/12-faithspirituality/270-americans-are-exploring-new-ways-of-experiencing-god. Copyright © by The Barna Group, Ltd.

3 Barna, George. *The Frog In The Kettle*. Regal Books, 1990.

4 John 18:37

Chapter 1: What People Believe

1 ABC News. "Nine in 10 Believe in Heaven; A Quarter Say for Christians Only." http://abcnews.go.com/images/Politics/994a1Heaven.pdf. Copyright © 2005 by ABC News.

2 Adherents.com. "Major Religions of the World Ranked by Number of Adherents." http://www.adherents.com/Religions_By_Adherents.html. Copyright © 2007 by Adherents.com.

3 Ibid.

4 John 14:7

5 Adherents.com. "Largest Religious Groups in the United States of America." http://www.adherents.com/rel_USA.html. Copyright © 2005 by Adherents.com.

6 Lifeway Christian Resources. "Unchurched Americans Turned Off by Church, Open to Christians." http://www.lifeway.com/Article/LifeWay-Research-finds-unchurched-Americans-turned-off-by-church-open-to-Christians. Copyright © 2007 by Lifeway Christian Resources.

7 Adherents.com. "Largest Religious Groups in the United States of America." http://www.adherents.com/rel_USA.html. Copyright © 2005 by Adherents.com.

8 The Pew Forum on Religion & Public Life. "'Nones' on the Rise." http://www.pewforum.org/Unaffiliated/nones-on-the-rise.aspx. Copyright © 2012, The Pew Forum on Religion & Public Life.

9 The Pew Forum on Religion & Public Life. "U.S. Religious Landscape Survey." http://religions.pewforum.org/reports. Copyright © 2008 by The Pew Forum on Religion & Public Life.

10 Barna Group. "A New Generation Expresses its Skepticism and Frustration with Christianity." http://www.barna.org/barna-update/article/16-teensnext-gen/94-a-new-generation-expresses-its-skepticism-and-frustration-with-christianity. Copyright © 2009 by The Barna Group, Ltd.

11 Patterson, James, and Peter Kim. *The Day America Told The Truth*. Prentice Hall Trade, 1991.

12 Gallup, Inc. "Religion." http://www.gallup.com/poll/1690/religion.aspx. Copyright © 2011 by Gallup, Inc.

13 Centers for Disease Control and Prevention. "Prevalence of Sexually Transmitted Infections and Bacterial Vaginosis among Female Adolescents in the United States." http://www.cdc.gov/stdconference/2008/press/summaries-11march2008.htm. Copyright © 2008 by Centers for Disease Control and Prevention.

14 Centers for Disease Control and Prevention. "Birth Data." http://www.cdc.gov/nchs/births.htm. Copyright © 2009 by Centers for Disease Control and Prevention.

15 Barna Group. "Da Vinci Code Confirms Rather Than Changes

People's Religious Views." http://www.barna.org/barna-update/article/14-media/153-da-vinci-code-confirms-rather-than-changes-peoples-religious-views. Copyright © 2006 by The Barna Group, LTD.

Chapter 2: Factors Which Affect Beliefs
1   2 Timothy 4:3
2   Revelation 3:15-16
3   1 Corinthians 13:12
4   Inside Higher Ed. "Not So Godless After All." http://www.insidehighered.com/news/2006/10/09/religion. © Copyright 2008 Inside Higher Ed (www.insidehighered.com).
5   Proverbs 11:2
6   Proverbs 13:10
7   Proverbs 16:18
8   Revelation 3:17
9   Hebrews 6:18
10 John 14:9
11 John 4:24
12 1 Corinthians 2:14
13 Jeremiah 1:5
14 Ecclesiastes 12:7
15 Luke 18:25
16 Proverbs 3:5
17 Exodus 33:19

Chapter 3: The Search for Truth
1   Unity. "Frequently Asked Questions." http://www.unityonline.org/aboutunity/whoWeAre/faq.html. Copyright © 2008 by Unity®. All rights reserved.
2   2 Timothy 3:16-17
3   Harpo Productions, Inc. http://www.oprah.com/books/favorite/slide/slide_books_favorite_05.jhtml - (viewed in September, 2008). Copyright © 2008, Harpo Productions Inc.
4   Butterworth, Eric. Discover the Power Within You. Harper & Row, Pub., 1968.

5   John 6:38

6   Luke 24:51

7   Hebrews 9:27-28

8   Matthew 24:23-25

9   Luke 21:34-36

10   Matthew 7:21-23

11   John 14:23

Chapter 4: The Sources of Truth

1   Barna Group. "Americans Draw Theological Beliefs From Diverse Points of View." http://www.barna.org/barna-update/article/5-barna-update/82-americans-draw-theological-beliefs-from-diverse-points-of-view. © Copyright 2009, The Barna Group, LTD.

2   Luke 1:34

3   Strobel, Lee. *The Case for the Real Jesus.* Zondervan Publishing House, 2007.

4   Acts 9:4

Chapter 5: What Do We Know About God?

1   Exodus 20:3

2   Genesis 6:6-7

3   Exodus 3:14

4   Ezekiel 36:22-23

5   Matthew 17:5

6   Genesis 1:27

7   Genesis 1:1

8   John 4:24

9   Matthew 11:27

10   Matthew 18:12-14

11   Matthew 19:26

12   John 8:28-29

13   John 3:16-17

14   Matthew 5:17

15   John 10:16

16   John 10:30

17   John 14:6-8

18 Matthew 10:32

19 John 8:58

20 Hebrews 13:8

21 2 Corinthians 5:21

22 1 John 3:8

23 Mark 16:6-7

24 Luke 24:50-51

25 John 14:3

26 John 14:6

27 Luke 2:26

28 Luke 11:13

29 John 14:26

30 Romans 8:26-27

31 Acts 1:8

32 Acts 2:4

33 Acts 2:38

Chapter 6: What Are Angels?

1 Graham, Billy. *Angels.* A Crossings pub., 1994.

2 Genesis 6:1-2

3 Colossians 1:16

4 Genesis 19:5

5 2 Peter 2:4

6 Revelation 12:7-9

7 Daniel 10:7

8 2 Kings 6:15-17

9 Ephesians 2:10

10 Daniel 10:12-13

11 Acts 12:11

12 Daniel 8:15-17

13 Matthew 13:41-42

14 Matthew 18:10

Chapter 7: Is Chapter 7: Is Satan Real?Satan Real?

1 Barna Group. "Americans Draw Theological Beliefs From Diverse Points of View." http://www.barna.org/barna-update/article/5-

barna-update/82-americans-draw-theological-beliefs-from-diverse-points-of-view. Copyright © 2009, The Barna Group, LTD.

2 Ezekiel 28:12-17

3 John 8:58

4 Matthew 2:16

5 2 Corinthians 11:14-15

6 Isaiah 14:13-14

7 Matthew 8:29

8 Revelation 12:12

9 Matthew 4:3

10 Luke 4:13

11 Luke 8:12

12 John 13:2

13 Job 1:6-7

14 John 13:27

15 Genesis 6:1-6

16 Matthew 8:28

17 Mark 1:32-24

18 Luke 8:33

19 Matthew 8:29

20 The Pew Forum on Religion & Public Life. "'Nones' on the Rise." http://www.pewforum.org/Unaffiliated/nones-on-the-rise.aspx. Copyright © 2012, The Pew Forum on Religion & Public Life.

21 1 John 4:2-3

Chapter 8: Spiritual Warfare

1 Matthew 7:21-27

2 Ephesians 6:11

Chapter 9: Summary of the End Times

1 Matthew 24:4

2 Matthew 24:36

3 Matthew 24:21

4 Matthew 24:29-31

5 Luke 21:9-11

6 United Nations. http://www.un.org/Pubs/chronicle/2005/

issue2/0205p20.html. – (viewed in September, 2008). Copyright ©
United Nations 2000-2008.

7   United Nations. "Global Food Security Crisis." http://www.un.org/
issues/food/taskforce/background.shtml. – (viewed in September,
2008). Copyright © United Nations 2000-2008.

8   Until There's A Cure Foundation. "Learn The Facts." https://until.
org/learn-the-facts/. Copyright © 2004-2008 Until There's A Cure
Foundation.

9   Matthew 24:14

10 Matthew 24:3

11 2 Timothy 3:1-7

12 2 Timothy 3:13

13 2 Timothy 4:3-4

14 Matthew 24:37-41

15 2 Peter 3:3-6

Chapter 10: Significance of the End Times

1   Revelation 13:11-17

2   Revelation 14:9-12

3   Revelation 13:2-4

4   Revelation 13:5-8

5   2 Thessalonians 2:4

6   Luke 16:19-31

7   2 Thessalonians 2:3-4

8   2 Thessalonians 2:7-10

9   Daniel 9:27

10 Matthew 24:15

11 Revelation 12:13-14, 17

12 Matthew 7:13

13 1 Thessalonians 4:15-17

14 Revelation 19:19-21

15 Revelation 20:1-6

16 Romans 11:25-32

17 Revelation 20:7-10

18 Revelation 20:11-15

19 Revelation 22:18-19

20 Matthew 10:32-22

Chapter 11: Conclusion

1 ThinkExist.com. ThinkExist.com ® is a web site containing thousands of quotations. Copyright © ThinkExist 1999-2013.

2 2 Timothy 4:3-4

3 John 3:17

4 Matthew 7:3

5 Lifeway Christian Resources. "Lifeway Resources Surveys Formerly Churched." http://www.lifeway.com/Article/LifeWay-Research-surveys-formerly-churched-part-1-of-2. Copyright © 2001-2013 Lifeway Christian Resources.

6 Ibid

7 Matthew 9:12

8 Matthew 7:23